The State of Grace:

A Mother's plea for life balance

P.G. MCGRATH

BALBOA
PRESS

A DIVISION OF HAY HOUSE

Balboa Press books may be ordered through booksellers or by contacting:

Balboa Press
A Division of Hay House
1663 Liberty Drive
Bloomington, IN 47403
www.balboapress.com
1 (877) 407-4847

Because of the dynamic nature of the Internet, any web addresses or links contained in this book may have changed since publication and may no longer be valid. The views expressed in this work are solely those of the author and do not necessarily reflect the views of the publisher, and the publisher hereby disclaims any responsibility for them.

The author of this book does not dispense medical advice or prescribe the use of any technique as a form of treatment for physical, emotional, or medical problems without the advice of a physician, either directly or indirectly. The intent of the author is only to offer information of a general nature to help you in your quest for emotional and spiritual well-being. In the event you use any of the information in this book for yourself, which is your constitutional right, the author and the publisher assume no responsibility for your actions.

Any people depicted in stock imagery provided by Thinkstock are models, and such images are being used for illustrative purposes only.
Certain stock imagery © Thinkstock.

Printed in the United States of America.

ISBN: 978-1-4525-1647-9 (sc)
ISBN: 978-1-4525-1649-3 (hc)
ISBN: 978-1-4525-1648-6 (e)

Library of Congress Control Number: 2014910252

Balboa Press rev. date: 06/25/2014

Contents

CHAPTER 1

File and Fly

11 April 2008 Madrid, Spain

> Love ought to manifest itself in deeds, not words.
> —St. Ignatius, *The Spiritual Exercises*

Some might say it's not terribly wise to spend a weekend with an old flame the day you are serving your husband a divorce petition, but I disagree.

"Grace, wait, wait… slow down, *despacio*," he said. "When did this happen?"

I looked up, away from the piece of luggage I was gripping like a security blanket, and right at him. "This morning."

He tossed his head back laughing—hard. Okay, as I write this and reflect a bit, it was very funny. Until yesterday, we hadn't seen each other in six or seven years. Yes, we spoke. We sent Christmas cards, the annual "how are you" call. Suddenly, here I was coming through his door, and before I could answer "how are you," I'd announced I had served my husband with a petition for divorce—that morning. Papers served while I was en route to the airport to get here. File and fly.

It was the expression on his face and the way he was laughing—the way only your former lover can laugh. A look that is a combination of sheer amusement and genuine affection all rolled into one. There's something very comforting about all of it: his warmth, his apartment, his humor. The past few months the current has completely challenged me, and now I have managed to swim into this fabulous piece of warm water. I slow down. I breathe easier. I have been walking on eggshells for months. It's okay now; I am at Pablo's, and he is grinning. Suddenly, I recall he always found me so amusing—that crazy *chica Americana*.

Pablo is twenty years my senior. Probably because of this, I take comfort in the look of amused affection on his face as he listens to me. Our age difference is another aspect of our relationship that has become more beautiful with time. I have discovered that every woman should have an ex who is twenty years her senior. That way, should she find herself single after years of marriage, she will be older but will still be twenty years younger than him. This is a beautiful thing.

When going through a divorce, there is great comfort in experiencing the fun that comes from being with a man. By the time you divorce, it has been a long time since you have experienced such fun. However, it can't be just any man. You're getting a divorce, and meeting someone new is time consuming. You can't let your guard down. You have to get to know the new person. This takes energy, an investment of time; yes, time—the Western world's most phenomenally precious commodity. You are painfully and literally aware of this, because you know how much your lawyer charges for her time. However, when spending time with someone who already knows you—who knows you speak too quickly, like the beach, and would die if forced to move to the suburbs—this is comfort. This must go in my divorce survival action plan: "spend weekend you serve spouse with an old flame—preferably a Latino for extra warmth." If nothing else, this gives you a chance to catch-up with an old friend and finally stop dwelling on why people believe marriage can work at all.

Anyway, Pablo knew. I told him a few weeks back, when we scheduled this weekend. There was the usual small talk—"My boys are fine," "Yes, I am still lecturing to US university business students," "Yes, it is very different from my days in New York practicing law," and "Classes are fine"—and then he asked how I was.

"I'm okay... I'm getting a divorce."

He paused and then sighed, "I'm sorry to hear that." There was a long pause, broken by "So when are you coming to Madrid?"

I suggested a date. No pause on my part. Hell, if it weren't for my boys, ages two and five, I would have asked him what he was doing for breakfast. The suggested day arrived soon enough, and here I am. Safe in Madrid, at Pablo's, while my soon-to-be ex-husband and boys are in London.

I moved my bags from beside the front door into the apartment. Pablo looked them up and down and then looked back at me.

"No, I'm not moving in. It's just I couldn't think while I was packing, so I packed everything."

He nodded his head and smiled. I sat down on the sofa. I noticed he had bought a new, or perhaps now not so new, piece of art for the big wall in the living room. If he bought it, it's something noteworthy. I wonder what happened to the other piece that used to sit on that wall. We talked.

He brought me a glass of water and reminded me to take a sip from time to time. I told him enough about what is happening. Pablo is a well-known journalist. While many people might be put off by having a drama told so quickly, he was not. He has built his life around listening to other people's stories and dramas. This is a man who, when Spain was on the verge of revolution in 1981, found a camera and the king so he could broadcast the now-famous historical speech in which King Juan Carlos denounced the coup attempt and declared his support for the Spanish constitution. This is a man who saved Spain. After saving Spain from Fascism, his brief role in my melodrama will be easy for him.

Still, the fact that he listened to the details of my divorce so patiently is impressive, given what is going on in his life. His beloved brother, Jose, is ill… very ill. In addition, Pablo has just left the media company he established twenty years ago. Pablo has never married—wise man—and work has always been the biggest part of his life. Really, he has just left his marriage, if you think about it. He discussed his decision to leave the media company briefly. Then he looked at me and said, "Are you hungry? You probably haven't eaten anything."

By the time he asked me it was already after eight o'clock—early for dinner here in Madrid—but I realized I was hungry; I had not eaten since the morning. Pablo suggested we go to a nearby restaurant.

"Guapa, vamos a comer."

He occasionally speaks to me in Spanish as a gentle reminder to not let all my Spanish slip. It's been too long since I've spoken Spanish. I came to Spain (as a university student) and first met Pablo fifteen years ago. Pablo and I have been friends that long now. He knew me when—long before I embarked on such ambitious roles as wife and mother and the places those would take me.

We walked a few streets of this city where I once lived, years ago. I can't believe I forgot how fantastic Madrid is. Madrid has such a unique quality of life—it's the people, the food, and how terribly chic Madrid is in its own singular way. I spent time in southern Spain years ago as well. While lovely and warm—with the most delicious oranges I had ever tasted—it could not compete with Madrid to me. Just as I was remembering how great Madrid is, a young woman walked up to Pablo and asked for directions to a *calle* (street). I looked at her and noticed she was well groomed, well dressed, not overly made-up but not without makeup, and had a fantastic bag and shoes. Both the bag and shoes were an exquisite combination of leather and suede. She walked away, and I said to Pablo, "A typical Madrileña, no?"

"Exactly—*tipica*. How do you say in English, a prototype?"

For a Madrileña, it's the clothes, bag, and shoes—especially that bag—that signal her origins. For a Parisian woman, it's the scarf. It's been over a dozen years since I'd last been to Madrid, but once you live in a city you never forget some things.

I rambled about my unraveling marriage. The divorce is complicated because of my past illness and some insurance money that's involved. I am worried about the apartment, the soon-to-be "marital home," as my lawyers are calling it. I mentioned one good thing is that Victor (my husband) travels often for work, so he is absent a lot. This was part of the challenge, however, of serving my divorce petition. I explained how I'd found myself hoping my husband would be in his office today, for once, so I would not have to pay (yet again) for someone to attempt to serve him with my divorce petition. People never talk about this aspect of seeking a divorce in the common-law system, but it is tricky having to find someone to serve your request for a divorce on your spouse. You actually have to have a live person serve the papers. I told Pablo I couldn't exactly ask my husband, "So are you in the office this afternoon? I really need to get the ball rolling on something that's been bugging the hell out of me for the past couple of years."

I explained a bit more about the logistics and why I found doing this not only emotionally but also technically challenging. In England, like in the United States, you have to find what is called a *process server*. A process server is a person who physically delivers documents to an individual involved in a court case, the idea being that a person has the right to know there are legal proceedings occurring against him or her. I was holding my breath hoping my husband had actually been in the office when the process server arrived to deliver the documents.

Other countries' legal systems don't require proof of service by a person to start a lawsuit. It's not like this in Spain. To think it all dates back to 1066 and William the Conqueror with the Normans in ancient England starting the legal system we have today: the common-law system. Didn't they come up with the idea of the *writ*—legal papers that had to be served?

I tell Pablo how even Roman Abramovich, Russian oligarch and owner of Chelsea Football Club in London, managed to avoid an English lawsuit issued by his former business partner, Boris Berezovsky, for ages. Berezovsky spent four years trying to serve papers on Abramovich. Miraculously, the papers were finally served when the two ran into each other one afternoon in London's Sloane Square at the upscale, high-end fashion retailer Hermès. That story has become legend—how Abramovich's former business partner tossed the legal papers to him saying, "I have a present for you." Later the shop's CCTV footage of the papers being physically served on Abramovich was used to demonstrate proof of service in court. Smile, Roman, you are on camera! Allegedly, Abramovich did not touch the papers, somehow thinking that would prevent the start of the lawsuit. All I know is that afternoon was a good one for Abramovich's lawyers; the Russian oligarch's legal Olympic games and Olympic-sized legal fees were about to begin. Hmm... not even a dodgy Russian can avoid the long arm of English law if he continues to live in London.

Of course, my annoying search to locate my husband means nothing in comparison to losing your brother. Pablo is close, so close, to his brother. Pablo and Jose shared an apartment years ago when Jose was still single. When Jose married, he and his wife moved into the apartment next door to Pablo's. They have lived next door ever since with their two boys. When I think of them, I remember something a friend of mine, who is a social worker, said: "A sibling relationship is usually the longest relationship most people have in their lives."

Forget the old school pals, your first roommate, your best man—your brother or sister knew you for years before those people arrived. Now, while some people may not think much of their sibling relationship or any familial relationships, others do. Jose and Pablo are prime examples. You can skip the spouse; Pablo is facing the reality of losing his best and oldest friend.

Eventually, I stopped venting about my marital problems and, frankly, suspended being the night's entertainment. I decided to ask about the real issue, the one I had been intentionally avoiding. "How's Jose?"

He looked at me and dropped his voice, "It's not good."

He provided just enough detail for me to deduce "it" was something malignant and bad. I told him my truth—I would do anything for a world without cancer. He knows that I lost a breast to it. Words can never fully describe the bubble you enter when the doctor tells you that you have the "c" word. As I sat there talking about my divorce, it dawned on me that many people find betrayal when friends or family members do something they never imagined they would: cheat, lie, steal, sleep with another person. I suspect this is most people's definition of betrayal. I, however, have another definition of betrayal; betrayal to me is when your own body turns on you—now that is betrayal. Can we ever really count on another human being? Don't we always know, somewhere inside our psyche, we are taking a gamble? But your own body growing an enemy inside you? You need your body. You don't *need* a person who betrayed you; that is an illusion that the perceived betrayal—the divorce, the affair, the lie, the fraud, the cheating, the abandonment—wisely smashes. By discovering it, you are on the first step to seeing the world more clearly, to gaining the truth. But illness... damn. I still miss that breast, although I am grateful I had the option to remove it so I could move on with life. I have lived to see another birthday with my beautiful boys.

"They need to do more tests," Pablo said. "He has appointments next week. We'll know more then."

The waiter arrived to take our order. While I had no doubt I needed a drink, I was so flustered I could not remember the Spanish word for sparkling wine. After an awkward silence, I mouthed while looking at Pablo, "Champagne?"

Pablo announced, "*Una cava para la senora... Ay, guapa*, you've been away too long."

He is right; I have been away way too long. While I did not consciously plan it, I could not help noticing that the synchronicity proved better than I ever could have imagined. This weekend—while I have formally and legally requested freedom from marriage—I returned to the first city I lived in outside the United States, my country of origin. There is something so powerful about living in a country outside your own. It alters your view of yourself and your own culture. After you live in another country, you are never the same person you were when you arrived in your new nation. The trick is you must live in the country, not simply travel through it. You must do mundane things, such as go to the post office, dry cleaner, and pharmacy. You must struggle in a language you do not speak well. Of course, when I lived in Madrid phone calls were more expensive, no one e-mailed, and cell phones were enormous devices used by a handful of people. I gained real space not interrupted by virtual contact.

We ate a delicious meal of fish and potatoes, common Spanish cuisine. As we walked back to his apartment, he asked about my plans for the weekend. He knows I will want to see my friends Alicia and Rosada and their mother, Maria. He asked if there is anything else I want to do while here. We stayed up late, but not too late, talking. As I write this I realize I slept better last night than I have in weeks. I slept well because here, at Pablo's, all is well for both of us—at least for now.

12 April 2008 Madrid

> Acceptance is the sense of belonging.
> —M.F. Moonzajer

Yesterday (Saturday) afternoon proved to be wonderful. I saw my Spanish "sisters," Alicia and Rosada, and their mom, Maria. They had me over for a delicious lunch at Maria's house outside Madrid, surrounded by a typical dry, arid Spanish landscape with a limited amount of trees. Maria reminded me that I will always be her *hija* (daughter) and gave me the warmest welcome imaginable.

We met seventeen years ago and have remained friends. Years ago I'd lived in Maria's apartment in Madrid, while Alicia and Rosada were studying at university. Maria rented the place to students, like myself at the time, so Alicia and Rosada could also stay there when needed. Needless to say, typical tenants paying the going Madrid rental rates would not have welcomed the landlady's young adult daughters dropping by whenever they were inclined.

I had not seen my friends in Madrid for years, while I embarked on the job of wife and mother. But I am here now, and it is like we were never apart. The weather was a perfect spring day. I met all the boyfriends, the husbands, and the children. They know I am getting divorced and, like good European friends, they asked about my summer holiday plans. They are all chartering a boat in Ibiza; would I like to join?

Maria, herself amicably divorced from Alicia and Rosada's father, had her current boyfriend there and was surrounded by her children and grandchildren in her fabulous home. You can't help noticing how great she looks. Maria has always been pretty, with shiny light brown hair and pretty, well-tailored clothes, right down to her jeans. What struck me the most was her loads of energy as she served food, played guitar with her grandchild, and joked often.

After lunch I came back to Pablo's for a drink with Pablo and his sister-in-law, Catherine, Jose's wife. While Jose stayed at home, Catherine very kindly stopped by Pablo's apartment from across the hall to say hello.

I like Catherine a lot. We have several things in common. We are both Americans from the New York area; she is from New Jersey, and I from New York. We both married Europeans and moved permanently to Europe. We both faced the challenge of having to build careers outside the United States. She has had a wonderfully successful career in insurance and raised her boys in a bilingual home. My boys are also bilingual, and I ended up leaving my career as a lawyer to become a business and law lecturer. Catherine asked me about life in academics, as she knows I lecture mostly to US university students in London. We talked about raising kids, who are Americans, outside their country of origin. She mentioned how fortunate I am that I don't lecture during the summer when I take the boys to New York. I reminded her that her career in insurance is far more financially lucrative than mine in academics, so there is always a trade-off.

Catherine told me that for a couple of years when her boys were younger, work brought her back to New Jersey, so they did get to experience living in the United States. She smiled, and I asked, "How old were your boys those couple of years?"

"They were old enough to remember their US years well," she said. I explained that, with the divorce, the country I decide to settle in is one

10

of the issues I am most concerned about. How will I support myself after the divorce living in Europe? I have already accepted the fact that my soon-to-be ex is based in Europe. If I were to move back to New York, the boys would not see their father often enough. I told Catherine that would not benefit anyone.

The most captivating part of our discussion was not, however, about our shared experiences as Americans and mothers outside the United States. What really struck me was when she said that, regardless of the results of Jose's tests, she knows that every day she and her boys—now young men at the university in Madrid—have with Jose is a gift. Jose is a great father and has always been really close to his sons. Though I have not seen Jose yet this weekend, somehow thinking about him gives me strength. Every day is a gift, and you can't spend it in a situation that is making you miserable. For me that situation is my marriage.

13 April 2008 Somewhere over Spanish Air Space

> The greatest burden a child must bear is the unlived life
> of the parents.
>
> —Carl Jung

Well, I am back on the plane to London and impressed I managed to board it. Late this morning at Pablo's apartment, I'd collected my things but I really didn't want to leave. Fortunately, Rosada had offered to give me a ride to the airport; this was helpful, because I am not sure if I would have had the interest or strength to find a taxi to take me. While I was packing, Pablo sat on his sofa, cigarette in one hand. With his other hand he made the motions of turning a key into a lock—a key that did not fit its fictitious lock. His face showed perplexity and frustration. For added effect, he then included sound effects, sounds of a key not working—"click, click, click, click."

"Thanks" I said with a look of exasperation. "Easy for you, since you never got married. You must be feeling terribly proud of yourself."

It is my default response to him, reminding him he never married. He smiled. "Yeah, close a couple of times, but—"

I knew where he was going with this, so I interrupted him, "What was it, two engagements? Of course, with the first one you managed to get the foreign correspondent job in New York while she stayed in Madrid. That was convenient. Always the career, my dear, always the career—your true love."

"Ah, sí, New York." He was grinning like a Cheshire cat, and I knew he was remembering those days of career fast-track glory. New York in the eighties, when Madonna released her first single and Keith Haring's art was for free on the subway.

"Besides, close does not count," I told him.

I have already decided marriage is not like horseshoes and hand grenades; "close" may bring you somewhere emotionally, but it does not bring legal fees, court calendars, and other new words I am learning, such as *decree nisi* versus *decree absolute*.

I looked at Pablo while standing over my open luggage and said, "So do you know the joke?" He looked at me with a "well, let's hear it" face. "What is the first step toward divorce?" I paused and then answered, "Marriage." He laughed.

"That one is cute," I said, "but my favorite is a saying I recently discovered." Again, I got the "let's hear it" face. "Love is blind, but marriage is a real eye-opener!" We both laughed as I announce, "I sure have learned that to be my truth."

As I finished packing, I looked around at his flat, at him, at my luggage, at the beautiful Spanish sunshine outside. I asked him how he thinks the next year is going to be. I often have looked to him for answers. This probably is, in part, due to our age difference.

He thought for a moment and said, "We both have challenges in front of us, *Guapa*. I think you will have a difficult year, and then things will be much better. Don't worry so much about the apartment, Grace. I promise the next time I go to London I won't see you living on the street. We are both starting new chapters in our lives."

I looked at him and said, "A part of me really doesn't want to go. If it wasn't for the boys—"

Just then, my phone rang. It was Rosada. She was downstairs in her car and ready to go.

"Okay, *vamos*," Pablo said. He went downstairs and said hello to Rosada. I had introduced them years before. They made polite conversation.

As I opened the car door, he kissed me good-bye and lifted his arm in motion to indicate I was to stay strong. I thanked him for such a wonderful time and said how great it was to be in Madrid again. As Rosada and I were about to pull away, I rolled down the car window and said for the third time this weekend, "Quit smoking!"

We got to the airport and I said good-bye to Rosada. I took a deep breath as I got out of her car. She offered to park her car and join me, but I declined. It was easier this way. I knew I needed some time alone to collect my thoughts. As I wandered around the airport, I realized something about my old friendships and why I ended up here—in Madrid, of all the places on earth—this weekend. It has all been very serendipitous. I am old enough to know there are no coincidences, and

I knew I would find what I so desperately needed: the love of my friends and my former lover.

For eighteen years, Pablo has called me *guapa,* gorgeous, and truly, genuinely meant it. Year after year, he has owned that term of endearment for me. He holds the belief that I am beautiful and has spoken those words from his heart. Anyone can call a woman beautiful, but can they actually mean it? Over the course of eighteen years, a woman—any human being—accumulates wear and tear. Yet still, *guapa.*

He is a friend who will allow me to arrive at his door an emotional wreck. Even better, he is a man with whom I can skip the use of language and rely on hyperventilation as my primary form of communication. In my wired, stressed state, his response will be purely to laugh, provide me with space, and say only "Ay, *guapa.*" It is through this response that I can be emotionally fed after years of starvation. A rational observer might question the wisdom of letting a disturbed American woman through the door, but not Pablo. Pablo enjoys my company, forgives my chaos, and finds humor in nearly every aspect of my life, including the fact that I can't manage to perform the simple task of packing a bag properly. For this one weekend, I did not have to be so strong. I did not have to be a professor, mother, housekeeper, cook, litigant/petitioner, or client. This weekend I was and am a woman, a friend, and—best yet—a prodigal daughter who can let others feed me. I came to Madrid because Pablo believes I am a beautiful woman and because I will always be Maria's daughter and Alicia and Rosada's friend.

I am so grateful for my old friends and for the fact that I have the resources to take a trip like this to Madrid. It wasn't always this way; for years, I did not have much help with the boys. In fact, it seems as if for several years I have either been pregnant and nursing—all while simultaneously running a hotel for my husband to call home. Though there is only a three-year age difference between my boys, I can honestly say it seemed that once my older son turned two I had a brief period during which I was able to be something other than mother and hotel manager, before I was pregnant again. Yes, of course, I wanted to be pregnant. Like so many women, I wanted children. What I will never fully understand is why, when a woman becomes a mother, does it become so difficult for her needs as a woman to be met? Conversely, when a man becomes a father, his children are seen as a beautiful addition to his life. A woman, however, spends the next eighteen years in a nonstop grueling marathon to be a woman as well as a mother. After becoming a mother, a woman will engage in a constant struggle to determine a balance between her child's emotional and physical needs and her own. It is as if you have stepped on the scales of justice, and you and your children must constantly move around to know how to get the scales even. Some days you will dance, and others you will drag around those scales. Of course, my struggle to find any balance had been further complicated by the fact that no sooner had my youngest son been weaned, at the age of one, than I discovered a lump in my breast. I was forced to reexamine my life.

I keep thinking about Pablo's brother, Jose. I confess death and not life after cancer was the first thing I thought about when I first heard my diagnosis. I have been given a second chance at life. This life that is not a dress rehearsal; this is your one shot. This realization forced me to grapple with the difficult questions I hadn't wanted to discuss with anyone—let alone myself. I have now summoned up the courage to do what I know I must do, and somehow, in doing it, I appear at an old friend's whose brother is dying of cancer. Jose's time left on this stage is shorter than mine. Although the decision to end my marriage has been difficult, I know it is right. I am getting a second act; not everyone gets that chance. Jose may be in his final act.

There is something empowering about getting a second act once you have questioned whether your life was a one-act play. There is also something very nerve-racking about it. You go from postponing things until tomorrow to never forgetting you could wake up in the morning and be told you have cancer. The flurry of information that follows: You are sick. You will need to meet some doctors *this week*. By the time you are finished meeting them, the next year of your life will be planned out for you. You learn what it really means to cancel everything in your calendar, to discover the lists you make are an illusion you create to keep yourself occupied and happy. You may think you are attending a meeting next month, but actually you'll be at chemotherapy. You'll be meeting new friends, such as nurses, oncologists, surgeons, radiologist, and, if you are lucky, physical therapists.

I say if you are lucky you get to the physical therapy. Jose will probably not be meeting a physical therapist. The physical therapists come at the end of the grueling experience of being a cancer patient. After you have endured treatments, you will have a new body you must get to know and learn how to operate. You are told to go to physical therapy, and the physical therapists will show you what exercises you will need to do. Physical therapists are second act characters.

Every day is a gift, I repeated this to myself and summoned up the courage to board this plane. I did not want the weekend to end, because returning to London means wandering into the unknown. The only things I am certain about at this point in my life are death, taxes, and now, legal fees. Ah yes, I have already accumulated legal fees this early in the process. Madrid was a great break from my routine of being mom and lecturing. I had a chance to be a little less responsible and a bit more myself—albeit myself on the emotional edge.

As I walked through Pablo's door, I must have looked like Pepa, from the famous Spanish film *Women on the Verge of a Nervous Breakdown.* In the film, Pepa liberates herself from an emotionally abusive lover with the words "I'm sick of being good" as she mixes a gazpacho cocktail with a Valium kick.

Even better was that Madrid seemed a million miles away from the small conference room in my lawyer's office where I have been spending my time recently, detailing the unraveling of my marriage.

That was the challenge of the past month back home in London. Telling my lawyers the story of how it all fell apart.

CHAPTER 2

Leaning In and "Unreasonable Behaviour"

14 March 2008 London

> Do not give what is holy to dogs, and do not throw your
> pearls before swine, or they will trample them under
> their feet, and turn and tear you to pieces.
> —Matthew 7:6 NASB

Tomorrow I have an appointment at my solicitor's office to provide a timeline of my marriage—better said, to provide my proof of evidence. I know I must go through with this. Part of me hates admitting that the marriage has failed. Newly married couples have the unrealistic expectation that theirs will be the one that lasts. They overlook the fact that half of all marriages fail. Quite reasonably, I believed in the fairy tale. I really thought Victor and I would be a couple who would make it. I never would have predicted our union would end up in me experiencing such alienation… that it would poison me… that it would teach me being alone is far better than being with the wrong person. For years, I acted out the role of the martyr mother. I now must face the realization that the playacting almost cost me my life. My body is permanently scarred. The scar runs, appropriately enough, right across my chest. At least we have the boys; we did create these incredible people.

I kept lying to myself: things would improve when the boys were older, when his business was more established, when I went back to work, and so on. It was always another day in the future things would improve and my needs would start to be addressed. It took my illness for me to realize I was at the bottom of his list. I was so devoted to being what I thought was a "good wife," I was making myself sick with neglect. I ceased to exist. My entire life seemed to be based around serving him and our children. Perhaps that works for some women, but it has taken me too long to realize it does not serve me.

Whenever I get sad about ending the marriage, I think about one of the only times in my adult life I can recall feeling genuinely humiliated. It was a moment that lasted only a few seconds but left a lifetime impression on me. It was a wake-up call.

While I was in the hospital after my mastectomy, I needed to learn a series of arm stretches to assist my recovery, especially for the area under my armpit where some lymph nodes had been removed. A nurse was going to demonstrate the stretches in a conference room on the hospital floor. I walked over to the room, intravenous still by my side, and opened the door. In the room sat three other women, all in hospital gowns. The woman all looked at me and, instantly, I was slammed— hit hard by the unique combination of intense horror and pity in their faces. One woman even gasped audibly. Their thoughts were empirical: she is way too young for this disease. I was receiving pity from a room full of women with breast cancer. This was the bottom of the barrel. I, who when entering a room full of strangers was more accustomed to announcing my title and what the strangers were going to learn ("I'm Dr. Purdy, and this is Business Law."), held on to my IV and felt their horror. I was still reeling from the shock of their reaction when, after several seconds, I realized they were all seated around a conference table. After taking a seat, I allowed myself a moment to wonder how much younger I was than the other women, but then I caught myself. It didn't matter how much younger I was. I was here now and needed to learn these stretches.

Just when I thought my status couldn't get any lower, one of the women turned to me as we awaited the nurse. She was a pretty redhead, had a friendly manner, and was about fifty-something in age. She smiled, made polite conversation for a minute about the hospital, and then she asked me the question she really wanted to know: did I have children?

"Yes," I replied.

"Hope you don't mind me asking," she said. "How old are they?"

"One is four, and the other is fifteen months old."

She closed her eyes for a second and shook her head back and forth slightly. She then opened her eyes and made a face that clearly read, *I thought my life was difficult, but yours is really hell, sister.* I knew immediately she must be a mother by the look on her face, so I asked, "How old are yours?"

"Sixteen and eighteen."

There was a short pause that I had to fill because the heaviness of her sympathy was pulling on me. "Does your eighteen-year-old drive now?" I asked. I wanted to change the topic and remind her that there are always challenges.

She smiled. "Yes, he just got his license, and he wants a car. You have time before that one."

That brief conversation with this fellow mother and patient revealed so much to me. I know deep in my heart that all my education, my worldly travels, my ability to speak a couple of languages—these are just accessories I wear or tools I use. My sophistication is my favorite accessory, which fits neatly into that bag of tricks I take with me around the world. It accessorizes the costume I wear: the Superwoman costume. I can do it all—lecture, teach, raise the kids, breastfeed on demand, cook, clean, be the perfect friend, manage my finances, do property deals—all without a partner. All without family support. Why, I don't even need a nanny, just a cleaning lady a couple times a week, thank you, and, of course, a legal team to sort out the marital mess.

I usually don't list my yearlong hospital stay for chemical therapy and radiation treatments when recounting my travels, but it is probably the trip where I learned the most. I compromised so much of myself, I lost my voice and said it was all in the name of what was "in the best interests of the children." Ironically, losing their mother would not be in their best interest. We all agree on that.

Sometimes I wonder if my life would be easier if, like many people, I simply refused to see the injustice. My blood boils when I see these injustices and no one wants to acknowledge them. I feel like women are getting sick and slaughtered, but no one cares—not even other women. I mean, some women can do it all so effortlessly; we love that myth. To this day what makes me so angry was my husband's and the rest of society's refusal to recognize how hard I was working to raise our boys.

It's the myth that hurts women. We are told to "lean in" more, multitask... that with a bit more effort we can balance career and family. Once we do that, we can become "role models." But the truth is it does not matter how smart or talented a woman is—it is never enough according to Western culture. There is always room for more "improvement."

I also know why I so easily fell victim to this myth. My parents were so self-involved that I ended up mistaking healthy self-esteem for narcissism. I never wanted to make the mistakes my parents made, so I ignored my need for self-worth in an attempt to avoid becoming narcissistic. By doing this successfully, however, I managed to convince myself that my only value was in being responsible, dependable, and working to take care of everyone else's needs. Once my children arrived, I had no idea how to balance my needs, or their father's needs, with my own. Being like this and not putting any of my needs on the priority list attracted people and events into my life that ran me over. I could devote myself to others but not to myself. I wanted to be that fictitious superwoman. I believed if I could be a superwoman, then I could be loveable.

Well, now I know a bit better. I know we all get only twenty-four hours in a day and what we do with those hours varies tremendously. I just wish women would stop pretending "having it all" was achievable. I also know life as a single parent won't be easy, but it has to beat being married to a man who never looks at you as anything other than his servant.

15 March 2008 London

> Beware the ides of March.
> —William Shakespeare, *Julius Caesar*

Most of today was spent in a small conference room at my lawyer's office in Holborn. You know London has become your home when, in the midst of a crisis, you find yourself feeling happy because it is not raining. When I needed a mental break from the questions, I would gaze out the window, focusing on the gray London winter skyline where I could see the Gherkin and the London Eye in the distance. It took several hours to provide my lawyer with the timeline of my eight-year marriage and its breakdown. It starts out as a love story about two people from opposites ends of the Atlantic who meet at a wedding; by the end of the not so fairy tale, I am describing my visits to a cancer hospital. In the movies, I would have simply died and the film would have ended. Maybe I wouldn't have died, but the film would have ended with me bald and spewing out some piece of absolute rubbish about the experience of illness being something "we" can grow from as a couple. Or better yet, that bullshit famous line from *Love Story* with Ali MacGraw and Ryan O'Neal: "Love means never having to say you're sorry." That has to be the dumbest line in the history of cinema.

The best part of my reality not being Hollywood is that there is a definitely a *Professor and the Prince: Part 2*. The one where she decides to stop living his way and finally thinks about herself. She gets a windfall of money from an insurance policy, banks it, and hires some of the top matrimonial lawyers in London. Have you seen that one? It's much better than the original. To get to the sequel, however, I had to provide the story behind my soon-to-be-filed divorce petition. The day unfolded as follows:

"Where does he think you are today?" Sandra asked the question. I was slow to reply. Like a good lawyer, she repeated the same question, but in a different way, "Your husband, Grace—where does he think you are right now?" It was and is a good question every matrimonial lawyer—or solicitor, as we call them in England—should ask.

"Lecturing, I guess. Frankly, I don't think he thinks about where I go."

I smiled for a second, thinking of Geena Davis in the role of Thelma in the film *Thelma & Louise*. Thelma's husband, Darryl, is more interested in watching football than in his wife's whereabouts when she calls to tell him that she is with her friend Louise. The audience knows little about Darryl beyond that he's a car dealership manager who can never tell his wife when he will be home and claims to work lots of nights.

Darryl does, however, began to take interest in his wife when the FBI come to his house to inform him that she has been involved with a known criminal named J. D., played by none other than a young Brad Pitt. The authorities ask Darryl to come to the police station to collect Thelma. Down at the station, a handcuffed J. D. walks right past Darryl and says, "I like your wife." Darryl suddenly leaps out of his seat and tries to hit J. D.

While armed robbery sounds like an awfully complicated way to get attention and would do nothing but harm, especially to my boys, I could not help wondering if I could take a road trip to discover someone who looks like a young Brad Pitt. I would be especially interested in a man who bears a strong resemblance to the young Mr. Pitt around the abdominal area.

"We'll need a timeline of your marriage to help us gather your proof of evidence for the divorce petition. You will have to provide a lot of information. Some of the information will be routine, but some will not be. We will need details to prepare your case. I warn you, sometimes our clients find this process difficult." She paused for a second. "Okay?"

Sandra may be the more junior of the lawyers I've hired, but she is good. I like Sandra, what little I know of her. The lawyer in me likes that she worked in the family courts before she went into private practice. When I hired the senior lawyer and partner in charge, Anne, we agreed to have Sandra do as much of the work as possible because her billing rate is lower.

"I understand."

"So, how did you meet your husband?"

"At an old friend's wedding—I know, so cliché."

As I continued, it seemed peculiar to hear myself explaining to this stranger about how my soon-to-be former husband's brother married Alyce, an old university friend of mine from California. At the time, I was practicing law in New York City, so I'd crossed the country to be at the wedding.

Our first meeting hardly seemed like a decisive moment in either of our lives but for the fact he had flown in from Paris, in the company of his then girlfriend. I didn't know that so casual a meeting would have such long-lasting consequences.

"What happened next?"

"Not much. We chatted, we danced. He was there with his girlfriend at the time. I returned to New York, and he went to back to Paris."

Sandra's face showed she was waiting for an explanation. This could not be the end of the story or I wouldn't be paying hundreds of pounds an hour to sit in this conference room.

"The next time we met was about eighteen months later. I had planned to visit an old New York friend who was living in Paris, but my friend fell ill and decided she needed to return to the States for treatment. She needed some surgery and wanted to be near her mother, who lived in New York, for the two-week recovery time."

"I mentioned my disrupted plans to my friend Alyce, how I had booked a trip to Paris to see a friend who'd then suddenly decided to return to the States. Alyce suggested that I get in touch with Victor. After all, she pointed out, we'd chatted and danced at her wedding. I did get in touch, and we had a lot of fun. At the end of that trip, we said we'd try to see each other again soon. He came to New York a couple of months later, and from there we started dating. We traveled back and forth, spending time in both Paris and New York."

"That's how it all began—we did the long-distance thing. We were commuting between Paris and New York roughly once a month, though my trips to Paris were more numerous that his to New York. After a couple of years, we finally married in New York."

"You didn't live together before you were married?" asked Sandra.

"No. I quit my job a couple of months before the wedding and started spending more time in Paris. We didn't even live on the same side of the Atlantic Ocean, for that matter, before we were married." As I spoke, I could almost hear Ella Fitzgerald in her wry delivery of the song "A Fine Romance": "A fine romance, with no kisses... A fine romance, you won't nestle."

I felt the need to add an explanation as I watched Sandra type away. I realized on paper this whole thing would look insane. "You know, Sandra, Victor is funny, smart, and good looking. He's charming, educated, and he's so knowledgeable about the world. I mean, before I met him I couldn't tell you the difference between Senegal and Ethiopia. Okay, maybe I'm exaggerating a bit, but I certainly could not have understood the conflict a student of mine who is half Kuwaiti and half Syrian faces the way I do now. Victor made such an impression on me."

Just then there was a knock on the conference door. Sandra motioned for a man carrying a tray of tea and biscuits to enter. As soon as he left the room, I said, "You're busy typing. Why don't I pour us each a cup?"

"Thanks," she replied. "Milk, no sugar for me."

Somehow the act of pouring the tea made me feel more like I was with a friend and not my new lawyer. I continued my marital explanation, "Victor has a side that is wonderfully diplomatic; he understands different cultures. I work with academics, and you'd be surprised how many highly educated people are really very provincial. They don't ask big questions about the world. A lot of them aren't really that interested in teaching, let alone learning or engaging their students to challenge or question the status quo. Victor is interested in the world. I learned so much about the world from him. That's probably why I was able to leave my job and move to France."

Sandra then asked, "After the wedding in New York, you moved to Paris?"

"That's right. We lived in Paris for nearly a year. Because we were married, I was able to get my French residence visa. I applied because I had to have it to live legally in Paris—even though we'd already decided we were going to move to London."

"We talked about it before the wedding. In London, I'd be able to work. At that time my French was nonexistent, so there was no chance of working in Paris. It looked like fate when the French bank he was working for was bought by the English investment bank Darings."

"What was his role with the bank?" Sandra asked.

"He provides investment consultancy for major infrastructure projects in the developing world. Let's put it this way, Sandra, if you want to find funding for a bridge in Gabon, Victor's your guy. The English bank's new owners were moving a lot of the French bank's operations to London. He took time out of our honeymoon to negotiate his relocation package and salary in London," I explained.

When I told Sandra this, I recalled he had spent a lot of time on the phone during our honeymoon. Perhaps I should have seen this as a sign of things to come, but he'd frequently reminded me it was something he was doing for us. I was to hear a lot about what he was always doing for "us" as the years went by. He was always sacrificing our shared present for some random date in the future.

We sound terribly cosmopolitan, I realized as I heard myself speaking. I told Sandra how I'd grown up in New York with my brother. My husband, Victor, had grown up in France and West Africa, as the family moved to keep pace with the requirements of his father's job with the French government. Victor has three siblings. His two younger siblings were born in Senegal.

Sandra moved on to our life in London before the boys were born. It sounded a little defensive even to me when I told her that I'd always had a pretty independent social life. It had all worked fine.

"Then I became pregnant with our first child, Thomas. Surviving morning sickness was somewhat challenging, but by the fourth month it was behind me. My husband continued to support us at a distance, as he was still traveling. I did have my friends to call on," I said. "We decided we should use the time while I was pregnant and not working to buy rather than remain in the rootless condition of tenants. Once I was feeling better, I started to search for 'our flat'—then I found it."

I told Sandra that I thought the flat could be of real value. The location was great, as it was on a quiet street in Kensington. The flat, however, had suffered three decades or so of neglect. This was reflected in the price and explained why we could entertain affording it.

"Victor agreed that it would make a good investment, but he made it clear it was my project to manage. He was able to organize most of the financing, because he was an officer at Darings. We attended a couple of meetings together at the bank. Once we got the mortgage, I went to work hiring an architect and a builder. At one point the building work ran over budget. Victor asked his parents for a loan to cover the costs, and they did give him the money. The flat was ready about five months after our son was born. It was fabulous when we moved in. I finally felt more settled."

I continued our story, explaining how I went back to work when our eldest son, Thomas, was about a year and a half. "I took a full-time post with a large legal headhunting firm. To do the job, I needed to meet traders and lawyers who only wanted to speak with a headhunter during off hours. I often had to call them at home late at night or early in the morning or meet them at odd hours when they might be able to escape their desks for an hour or so. My husband's itinerary was as busy as ever. The nanny we'd hired was getting very upset with the increasingly long hours we required of her. I came to the realization that if I didn't give up the job, a nanny would be raising our son."

"Did Victor accept that you needed to give up the job?" Sandra asked.

"I thought so."

"Okay, so you went back to staying at home?"

"Yes, and things seemed to be getting a bit easier once Thomas turned two. He started going to a nursery school a couple mornings a week, and I had a babysitter help a couple of days. So with me home, we decided it would be a good time to try for another child. Victor surprised me when he returned home from work one day and told me about a conversation with a colleague at the bank. The colleague had said something about how he and his wife waited five years to try for a second child, and they were now having trouble. He asked Victor if we wanted another child and basically said something to the effect of 'don't leave it too long, because there is never a perfect time to have a child.'"

I stopped speaking to collect my thoughts. After the short silence, I said, "That's when I became pregnant with our second son, Rex. That's also when things started to really go awry. I mean, it may not sound logical, but I really thought things were better."

She saw I was struggling and starting to rationalize. As I heard the story aloud, I was feeling obliged to explain the decision to have a second child.

"It's just that—" I cut myself off. "You know, I guess I didn't realize how bad it was."

Sandra interrupted, "Grace, please stop being so critical of yourself. You know, this is so common. In family law we say 'one child is a hostage to fortune; a second is an insurance policy.'"

I smiled. "Yes, exactly. It just seemed so natural. We wanted to complete our family, and there is no perfect time in life for a child. Everyone knows that. Nevertheless, after our second son, Rex, was born, things—from my perspective—went from bad to worse."

Sandra pressed me for details. She paused, and I could no longer hear the laptop keyboard humming away.

"Have you ever heard that quote by Nora Ephron, the American writer, about children being an explosion?" I asked. "She said something like 'When you have a baby, you sent off an explosion in your marriage... the marriage becomes different.' I feel like Thomas was a firecracker, but Rex was the explosion for us. Ephron says the marriage becomes different, not necessarily bad or better, simply different. But for us..."

I paused again to reflect. I can't imagine my life, let alone the world, without Rex. He is an incredible little pistol of a kid, and I would do it all over again. I was struggling with how best to describe the impact of his arrival when Sandra summarized it brilliantly. "Marriage is like a bridge, Grace. It connects the parents. But sometimes the weight of what it is carrying can cause structural damage. I see it all the time in my practice."

"Yes, exactly. Sometimes you can repair the bridge, and sometimes it has to be torn down. This explosion caused severe structural damage. Well, there had been signs before Rex, but I kept telling myself it was because Victor was so busy launching his business." I thought back on the isolation of that period. "We never went out together—I mean *never*. He would never commit to social engagements. He always said he never knew when his work commitments would intervene. One year on our wedding anniversary, while I was pregnant with Rex, he was actually in town but insisted he had to go back to the office after dinner. Victor stayed at dinner for an hour and a half. Since my morning sickness meant I was having difficulty keeping food down anyway, I rationalized that one easily. It was not the best time for me to realize that I had made a critical mistake."

She asked me about coping with pregnancy and two-and-a-half-year-old Thomas. I still find it hard to convey to her or anyone else how keenly I felt my isolation. "I had some part-time babysitters during my pregnancy and after Rex's birth. Looking back, I have no idea how I did it given I nursed the baby on demand while my husband was seldom around. I was alone with the babies every night. Victor was still building up his business. That meant that we couldn't afford to employ a nanny. He rationed time even more rigorously than money. His long hours and constant traveling justified my solitary confinement. It was still all for 'us.' He said that we couldn't afford a babysitter for me to go out in the evenings. On the couple of days I had help during the week, I would get my haircut or go to the dentist, basic things like that." After telling Sandra this, I added, "Once Rex was a few months old, I decided to go back to work as soon as I could so I could have some respite from the emotional and physical strain of being on my own so often with the boys."

Sandra asked, "So how old was Rex when you went back to work?"

"He was about ten months old and still being breastfed, but only once in the morning and once at night," I replied.

I continued providing Sandra the details. I told her how my constant friend, Phoebe—who was a lecturer of psychology at a nearby university—suggested the idea of part-time lecturing to me. I mentioned the university to my flat neighbors one day in passing, and they happened to know people there too. So my neighbors and Phoebe both put me in touch with some people at the university.

Fortunately, my first lecturing job was very close to the flat. When I started teaching, I discovered I really enjoyed both the work and the reconnection with the world outside of the house. "The full-time nanny then became only marginally more affordable, because my lecturing doesn't cover her costs." As I told Sandra that, I made a face again.

"What does that face mean?" Sandra responded to my expression. "Is there something else I should know?"

"Not really, but somehow I believed that my salary should be enough to cover childcare costs. I never questioned why Victor could not meet it from his earnings, given how often he was away and at work. Anyway, thank goodness for the lecturing. It helped me a lot, but not enough to stop our marriage from sinking."

When I think about our marriage, I am amazed at my docility. Hearing me tell the story aloud today really solidified my amazement.

There I was, running the house on my own, buying the children's things, working part time, nursing the baby at night, cooking, cleaning, and paying the bills. God, I remember how the mail would pile up because I just didn't have the energy to look at it.

We had no sex life. I asked him to try counseling—which he resisted at first, but finally we did attend a few sessions. I got to that point in our story and then said to Sandra, "Then everything blew up."

"What do you mean?"

"That's when I found a lump in my breast."

"Okay, when was this?"

"During the summer after Rex turned one, just before I was due to return to the university for lecturing. I think it may have been there for some time, but because I was nursing Rex my breasts were enlarged and I didn't feel it. I noticed it about six weeks after I stopped nursing him."

"How did your husband react?"

"Victor deals with crises well. He was calm and collected about it and very concerned for the boys and me. After this, he started spending more time with the Rex. He was always devoted to Thomas."

"Is that when you decided to have treatment in New York?"

"Yes. After I was diagnosed here in London, I met with doctors in New York. The treatment was the same, but my decision to stay in New York, frankly, was due to the help of an old friend of mine. The friend, Ted—an old school chum—had a small apartment in New York in the building opposite my father's. At the time, Ted was living in Germany, so he only used it occasionally when he visited New York. He told me I could use his place for as long as I needed it. I knew if I stayed in London I'd never get to rest in our flat; I had been sleep deprived for years, and my children's claims on my time and attention wouldn't just go away. So I made the necessary arrangements."

"What were those?"

"It wasn't simple. Victor and the nanny we'd recently hired took the boys to New York. There the boys and the nanny moved in with my father. Victor managed to find a school for our older son, Thomas, to attend. My father took him to school every morning. Then I had to meet with an immigration lawyer to get a temporary visa for our nanny so she could remain in New York for the treatment period. I slept across the street at Ted's. My husband would come in and out of New York a lot."

"How did the boys respond to the move?"

"Well, Rex was too little to understand. But for Thomas, I think the time there was an unexpected bonus. He got to know New York, and he and my father became close. It turned out to be the silver lining in the cloud.

I started smiling. I asked Sandra a question, "Do you know who Martha Stewart is?"

"I've heard of her. She's a cook, right? Didn't she go to jail?"

"Yes, but she's big in the States, and not just as a cook. She is a type of doyenne of domesticity. She has a TV show, magazine, website—all about matters related to the home like cooking, crafts, housekeeping. When I was in treatment, I used to watch her daytime show a lot. One day, Thomas was home with me on a school holiday and Stewart's show was on. Thomas was playing with this toy car in front of the television. I asked him to move because I couldn't see the screen. I was like, 'Thomas, I want to see what Martha's cooking.' Thomas doesn't even look up from his car, and he says, 'Mom, why did Martha go to jail?' That threw me off guard. Before I could even answer, I was wondering, *How on earth did Thomas hear about that?*"

"Wasn't it insider trading?" Sandra asked.

"Actually, she got off on the insider trading charges. The feds got her on obstruction of justice—she'd told her secretary to tamper with the phone log. Anyway, I couldn't believe Thomas knew about her criminal record. I nearly fell off the sofa when he said that. That whole winter I'd been depicting her as the friendly lady on TV. I didn't feel the need to expose the child to her ex-con/felon side. Of course, my first thought was he heard it at school, but I couldn't help thinking, *He goes to a French school, and those French kids and their parents are not interested in Martha. She's an American thing.* So I said, 'Thomas, I'll answer that, but I want to know—how did you hear about Martha's time in jail?' He said, 'Grandpa told me on the bus going to school. Her picture was on the front page of the newspaper, and I told him we watch her show. He said, "Did your mom tell you Martha's just got out of jail?"' At this point I was trying to bide time because I had no idea how to explain insider trading to Thomas. Any lecture I could come up with regarding fraud on the market theories was going to be a bit too sophisticated for a four-year-old. So I just asked him, 'Did Grandpa tell you why she went to jail?' I'll never forget his answer. Thomas said, 'Yeah, Grandpa said the judge told her she took money that wasn't hers, so he sent her to jail.'"

"Not bad," Sandra commented as she was typing.

"I thought the same thing. The reason I mention this is to give you an idea about Thomas. He definitely was getting a different perspective on the world as a consequence of spending time with my father. I realized by the age of four and a half, Thomas had learned indirectly that getting your face on the front page of the *Wall Street Journal* is not a crowning achievement in life." I paused for a second and then added, "I'm sure it was the *Journal*, since that's the paper my father gets every morning. That's what he reads when he is not watching Fox News."

"Okay, let me backtrack for a second. You have mentioned your father a couple of times since we met. Does he still live in New York?"

"Yes."

"You grew up in New York—correct? Your whole childhood was spent there?"

"Yes, from birth to age eighteen, until I went to the university. Then I moved to Washington, DC, where I did my undergraduate work."

"What about your mother? Are your parents together?"

"No, my parents were together until I was about sixteen. They split toward the end of high school—secondary school, as we say here."

"May I ask what your mother does for a living?"

"Sure. She worked for the City and State of New York for most of her career, in a variety of jobs with different administrative agencies. But she is retired now. Before her local government career, she was a model."

"Does she still live in New York?" Sandra asked.

"No. After she and my father split, she took early retirement with her State pension and moved to Florida. She lives there with her current husband. After the divorce, she retreated from her old life. Neither my brother nor I hear from her much. I think she had been unhappy in New York for a long time."

"Okay, got it. So, as you were saying a moment ago, you and the boys along with the nanny moved to New York, staying at your father's and your friend's flat across the street. Your husband came in and out a lot. So is that how things were until your treatment ended?"

"Well, almost."

She waited.

"Money was still really, really tight. My husband had new constraints on his business to deal with because of spending time in New York while most of his business is in Europe and Africa. That was one challenge. Then Thomas's school, the one he had attended in London, claimed they were sorry but informed us that they wouldn't guarantee his place for the next academic year unless we paid for the current year. The school insisted we had to pay tuition for Thomas even though he was absent the entire year. We tried to get out of it, but we got nailed with that school. We managed to find the funds to pay the school, but that left us the problem of paying for the school in New York. I explained the situation to my father, and he paid most of the tuition for Thomas for the New York school that year. Things were so stretched financially—it was stressful. To release some pressure, I decided we had to rent out our flat in London."

"What did your husband say?"

"He couldn't deny that we had no reliable stream of income between us, so he did agree but, once again, he told me I had to make all the arrangements. I got my friend Phoebe and a former cleaner who brought her husband and another friend to pack up the flat and get it ready. They put everything in storage. Phoebe took the important documents, like the children's birth certificates, and my other friend, Liz, took the couple of things that were of any value." I smiled weakly when I told her this and shook my head. Sandra looked perplexed.

"I remember Phoebe told me while she was packing up my neighbor came out in the hallway. My neighbor asked why Victor wasn't there helping. Phoebe just said, 'I don't know. You'd have to ask him.' Even when the tenancy finished, he resisted having to collect the keys and meet with the estate agent or anything like that. He complained about a work conflict he had that day but, meanwhile, the flat was the only real income we had at the time. He even sent the agent an e-mail saying he had work constraints; he said he only had an hour, or something like that."

"He was traveling?"

"Yes, as always."

"Can you give me a sample of what a monthly travel itinerary for him looks like?" Sandra asked. "I'm trying to get a picture of how often and where he travels."

"He usually leaves on a Monday, sometimes a Sunday evening. He may go somewhere like Cameroon or Morocco, returning on a Friday. He travels to Francophone Africa mostly but not exclusively. Sometimes he meets his clients in Paris, which makes the traveling easier on him."

"He does this every week?"

"Not every week, but I'd estimate eighty percent of the fifty-two weeks a year. Things are quieter around New Year's and during August."

"Do you have a copy of that e-mail to the estate agents citing his tight time window somewhere?"

"Yes—do you want me to send you a copy?"

"Please."

"Okay, I'll find it. Anyway, I can't believe I was then dumb enough to pay off the mortgage."

"You mean how you paid off the mortgage via the critical illness insurance policy?"

"Yeah, another windfall for him. I wish him luck finding another wife who will pay off his flat for him."

"No, now stop that." She ceased typing and looked up from the computer, staring right into my eyes. "You paid it off because you are a good person; that's why you did it. Grace, I'll need to understand the details of the critical illness insurance policies—those are important— but before we get to that, let's finish the timeline and the tenancy. So the tenants moved out, and you returned to London—is that correct?"

"Yes, last summer. The local estate agent had found some people who needed to move somewhere for a few months after they had sold their place while renovations were being completed on their new home. The timing worked out well. They left this past July, and we returned about two weeks later."

"How were things once you returned home?"

"Well, understandably, my husband seemed very relieved to be back home. Things between us remained critical. He was back traveling and working. He lived in the flat as if it were a hotel; he still does. By Christmas, I realized nothing was going to change. That's when I accepted I had to leave. It was hard."

"Did you try to discuss the problems?"

"Often, but whenever I brought them up he'd say, 'You know how I feel. That's in the past. I don't want to talk about it.' He just cuts me off or tells me I am weak or always complaining. I think if you asked Victor for his side of the story, he'd tell you I should have continued working outside the home—even when the boys were infants. He'd tell you I didn't need to breastfeed them for all those months," I said, trying to keep the bitterness out of my tone. "The reality is he was never going to surrender his desire to run his own business. But this left me in a precarious state. We didn't have enough savings or much support from extended family. Victor's niece, Sasha, came and helped us a couple of times. She was great when we first returned home from the hospital after Rex was born. She also came to New York to help take care of the boys when our nanny was on holiday. She gave up her annual vacation time for that. Sasha is a star, but aside from her... it was tough. I mean, even when I tried to discuss some of the smaller problems, it was impossible. Victor has an answer for everything. I'll give you an example."

At that point, Sandra stopped typing and looked at me instead of the computer.

"Awhile back, I got on him for never taking public transport. Victor never rides the tube—I swear he has an allergy to traveling underground. Anyway, I said to him, 'You need to stop taking taxis everywhere. It costs a small fortune.' So you know what he said to me?"

"What?" Sandra had one eyebrow arched.

"He said, 'That's not true. I have a Nectar card.' I was so stunned by his answer, it took me a second before I burst out laughing."

Sandra was smiling. It was the only time I saw her really grinning today. It was funny. She said, "The Nectar card is the loyalty card where you earn points at the supermarket Sainsbury's right?"

"Correct. Frankly, I was surprised to learn he has a Nectar card. More importantly, he doesn't even know the name for the ticket we use on the underground. I said, 'Victor, you can't use a Nectar card on the tube. It's called an Oyster card.' Sometimes I don't know what planet he lives on. I mean, that's like asking American Express if you can pay your bill with your library card!" As funny as this was, I knew the seriousness of what it implied. "The sad part is, Sandra, when things become that farcical, you know you are in trouble. I mean, there is no point in staying married. We clearly don't want the same things. I know a lot of women stay married because they wonder about money, but it's so up and down with Victor's business. I'm always pushing him to release money from it."

It was then that Sandra said what I had been hoping for—we could break. "Well, we have a lot here, and I have a much better idea of timing now. Why don't we take a short break? I'll ask for some more tea and get some sandwiches sent up for lunch. You can stay awhile longer?"

"Yes, I don't have to be back till later."

"Good, because we need to maximize today. Let's break briefly."

When I got back to the room, Sandra was taking off her suit jacket. She was wearing a black-and-gray wool suit. It was warm in the small conference room, and I was glad I had not dressed too heavily. Perhaps I found the room warmer because I was sitting in the "hot seat."

She handed me a teacup, and I poured myself some tea. "Please tell me about the critical illness insurance policies," she said.

"Okay, both Victor and I took out critical illness policies when we bought the flat. They were relatively new—the idea being if one partner falls seriously ill, the other isn't left trying to figure out how to pay back the bank. The banks offer them when you take out a mortgage, along with life insurance. So we took one out for each of us. When I was in treatment, my husband asked me about the policies after someone at the bank suggested it might be applicable. He had been attending a meeting at the bank in London related to his business account. During that meeting, it came up why he was in New York so often. When he explained our circumstances, a bank officer asked if we had taken out critical illness insurance. I got in touch with the bank and started collecting the necessary documents. In addition to the documentation I had, I needed to get my doctor to write a letter. After reviewing the documents, the bank called me one day and said the claim had been approved. That's when the bank also told me I could either keep the cash or put the money toward the mortgage. I told them I would need to speak with my husband and would get back to them shortly."

"So you discussed this with your husband?"

"Yes, I spoke with Victor. We agreed to put the money toward paying off the mortgage."

"How much was the policy payout?"

I sighed. "Large, £505,781.00. That policy is one of the documents I brought today."

"Okay, so that is the first policy, correct?"

"Yes."

"Now, you told Anne and me the other day that there was a second insurance policy. Can you explain that?"

"Yes. When Victor told me he was leaving the bank and was going to be self-employed, I suggested we meet with an independent financial advisor. That was years ago, back when we first moved into the flat. Basically, if anything ever happened to him, I didn't want to be stuck trying to survive with the boys on a limited income due to me being home for years. So we met with an advisor who suggested we take out additional critical illness and life insurance policies on Victor. Then, during the meeting, he commented that if anything ever happened to me, Victor would need to pay a lot for childcare because of his extensive work traveling. So we decided to take out another critical illness insurance policy on me."

"That policy was for how much?"

"That policy was for two hundred thousand pounds. I cashed that policy once we returned to London and I realized I needed to move on the divorce."

"And that, I believe you told Anne, is how you are paying your legal costs, correct?"

"Yes, I am paying my fees through the second insurance policy. That policy was in my name only and not tied to anything we owned together. I can promise you Victor is not seeing these bills."

"Okay, so back to your flat for a moment. So do you now own the flat outright?"

"No. After we paid off the mortgage, things were fine for a while. But shortly after we returned to London, Victor said he thought it best we take out a new, albeit smaller mortgage. Again, he wanted to alleviate any pressure on the business. So I went along with it—and that is when I wonder what I was thinking. I mean, I was tired after my treatments, especially with the extra effort of moving back and rebuilding my body. Also, I didn't want to worry about money; I'd been doing that for years. I didn't have the energy to come up with another way to address our finances. This time we took out a mortgage for two hundred thousand pounds, which was a lot smaller than the old one. Still, I felt I could no longer trust Victor after we took out that mortgage. I told Anne that after that new mortgage I knew things would never change and it would always be about him and his business."

"So that mortgage of two hundred thousand pounds remains on the property today?"

"Yes."

Sandra nodded her head while she slowed her typing. I could see she was tapping the arrow keys and scanning the laptop screen. "Give me a minute," she said as she was gleaning the information. She took a couple of sips of tea while staring at the computer. She then looked over at the small pile of documents I had brought, including the ones regarding the insurance policies and the original mortgage.

I sipped my tea and waited for her to speak. She then looked up and said, "Okay, I want to go back to one earlier answer. When I asked you if your husband agreed with your decision to quit the legal headhunting job, you said, 'I thought so'—what do you mean by that?"

"Well, that decision came up in those couple of counseling sessions we had. That's when I learned that he was annoyed I hadn't gone back to work after I first had Thomas. But I didn't want to leave Thomas as an infant or have to prematurely wean him. I did go back to work when he was about eighteen months old, but it was hard. Some nights I got home as late as eleven o'clock, and I was upset Thomas was having to spend so much time with a nanny. I also felt unhappy because I did everything in the house and didn't feel Victor was pulling his weight. Some nights when Victor was in town and I had to work late and meet a lawyer or trader, he would go home and relieve the nanny but then go back to work when I returned or work from home. He felt he had to make up the time away from work. As a result, even when he was in town we never spent any time together."

"Okay, that answers my question. Did anything else come up in those sessions that you think we need to know?"

"No, it was mostly me pleading and Victor labeling it complaining."

"Okay, we are almost finished. Just let me look this over for a minute."

It had been a long day. We'd worked together for several hours with just a couple of short breaks. Still, a lot had been accomplished. Sandra had the entire history of the marriage, which she needed to draft a divorce petition.

She looked up at me. "Alright, I am going to review everything and then send it to you for a final review. I will mark the copy I send to you for any outstanding questions. Please change anything that is not correct. I've been typing as you speak, so there may be a couple of items that need correcting when you get my copy."

"Okay, I'll review it carefully. May I assume you thought it faster to type it up now, so we saved time and money?"

"Exactly, I didn't want to take notes and then charge you for the time spent typing them or going back and forth with my secretary when she might not be able to read something handwritten. This way, if you review it carefully, you'll be the one filling in the gaps. That will keep the cost down."

I was relieved to be able to go home. Telling the story had taken more from me than I anticipated. It also dawned on me that it is difficult to be the client—something I have never experienced until today. For someone who used to practice law and then moved into academia, it has been a learning experience switching to the client's seat.

Sandra assured me that the petition will not be served until I give the final go ahead.

45

"Grace, when you review this, remember we need to make the divorce petition strong enough that the court will grant you the motion. We are filing on the grounds of 'unreasonable behaviour,' and we must cite some of the examples of his 'unreasonable behaviour' so the petition can move forward. I realize you may not like sharing everything you had to today, but we need it for proof of evidence."

While I am not comfortable citing my husband's "unreasonable behaviour," everything I have written in my petition is true. The challenge has not been in finding examples of his "unreasonable behaviour" but in committing them to paper. I am paying hundreds of pounds an hour to draft a divorce petition, yet I am still fearful of upsetting my husband. It's crazy.

"Right." To clarify I added, "So we need to provide the court with examples, such as his inability to dine with me, as proof of his 'unreasonable behaviour.'"

"Yes, exactly. It needs to be strong enough the court will see why the marriage needs to be terminated."

"I understand. Still, I know Victor. Let's make sure the petition emphasizes he is a good father. In a funny way, that's one of the problems—he is really interested only in work and the boys."

What I did not say to Sandra is that somewhere along this road I ceased to be a woman or his lover. I am mother, nanny, cook, driver, property manager, and personal assistant. I am not a woman, but a servant. I feel like an actress who was miscast. *Hey, I'm not supposed to play the maid! My role was the leading lady. Get me a new script, damn it!* If only I found the role of diva as comfortable as martyr mother.

"Yes, we will make sure the petition states he is a good father. In the meantime, Anne has been looking into what issues might arise because of your different nationalities. We will have a final answer on that shortly. She was in court today with another client, so I couldn't reach her. Let me speak with her, and I'll get back to you about next steps."

I said bye for now to Sandra. As I left the building, I thought about "unreasonable behaviour." It's not the same as the American equivalent of "irreconcilable differences." It's different because technically the English courts require a spouse has grounds for the divorce. The spouse requesting the divorce must provide good enough examples of why the other spouse's behavior is so unreasonable that the court can see why the couple cannot stay married. You must show the court your marriage has "irretrievably broken down." This is not the same as having differences you simply can't reconcile.

An irretrievable marital breakdown was the foundation for the most famous of modern-day English divorces: the Prince and Princess of Wales. It is what Prince Charles famously declared in his BBC interview—his marriage to Princess Diana had "irretrievably broken down." He got those words from his expensive lawyers, trust me. His lawyers told him, "When the interviewer asks what happened, you say the marriage 'irretrievably broke down.'"

I am sure his lawyers also advised him to steer clear of the topic of his girlfriend of the past twenty years when discussing his irretrievable marital breakdown. His lawyers had the difficult position of explaining to their royal client that, in the modern era, it is not especially regal for a future king to marry one woman while he is seeing another.

I am not, however, in the unusual circumstance of being a future monarch who wants to divorce without having to relinquish the throne. I am a typical woman—a mother and caretaker who tried to be a good wife and who foolishly believed the more I took on, the more enamored he would be with me. I kept thinking the more I gave, the more I would get back. Why, oh why, did it have to take a disease for me to acknowledge the more I gave, the more I lost and the less I got in return?

CHAPTER 3

The Four Hundred Million Pound Man

27 March 2008 London

> For where two or three are gathered together in my
> name, there am I in the midst of them.
>
> —Matthew 18:20 KJV

"Dr. Purdy, why did she ask for thirty thousand pounds a year for wine when she doesn't even drink?"

That was my favorite question today in class. It started off a wonderfully animated discussion of probably the most famous of all English divorce cases to actually go to trial, James Paul McCartney and Heather Anne Mills McCartney. The thirty thousand pounds question is a good one. I like it for a couple of reasons. Firstly, my student is being irreverent while simultaneously showing respect for the class. You don't have to sit in my lecture hall for long to realize I rely on my sardonic sense of humor to teach. Secondly, the question demonstrates he has clearly read the assignment and is critically examining it with some intellectual curiosity—albeit not a classic kind. Still, this student wants to know why the court entertains these questions. After all, what type of legal system debates whether to allow a nondrinking litigant to ask for thirty thousand pounds a year to maintain her wine cellar as part of her postmarital "needs"? Lord, all I want to do is keep my apartment, my small home that is not even a house. However, I realize an apartment is a lot. After all, didn't Tina Turner ask for only a car and Ike's last name when she left? (Hey, it was California—the car was probably more critical than a home. You can't get to an audition without a car.)

I paused briefly and decided the best way to answer this question was to flip things around and put the student in our litigant's shoes. "Doug, do you drink?" (An empirical but, nevertheless, calculated question on any professor's part to nearly any UK or US university student.)

"Yeah."

"Okay, what do you drink?" (The real question, to which I did not know the answer.)

"Vodka."

"Okay, so when people come over to your place, is the only thing that you offer them to drink vodka?"

"No." His classmates were looking at him now, many of them flashing sly smiles.

"You ever offer them anything else—maybe champagne? You look like the kind of guy who might offer champagne."

He then saw my point and responded, "Only André—usually out of a funnel." Everyone was laughing, including me.

Sandra had mentioned McCartney and Mills McCartney in passing the other day when we were working on the timeline of my marriage. I had asked her for copies of a couple of the lead family law cases so I could read up on the law. She then said, "Of course, we are waiting for the McCartney decision to come down any day now. That should be of some interest."

I confess to first reading *McCartney* out of personal curiosity. To my delight, I realized I had stumbled upon a pedagogical tool. In an indirect way, the case does a brilliant job of teaching my business students the differences between types of alternative dispute resolution (ADR), such as mediation versus litigation—more commonly known as going to court or suing somebody. ADR has become very fashionable over the past several years, but it has serious drawbacks. The McCartneys' divorce trial provides a wonderful case study. Not, I suspect, that they were thinking about this when their marriage began unraveling. *Well, honey, if it all falls apart, at least we can jazz up some boring law lectures.*

After Doug's funny question, another student said, "This whole thing was a waste. She was being greedy."

"Really, you think so?" I posed a question to the entire lecture hall: "How many of you think she was being greedy? Who thinks Ms. Mills was greedy, or may I rephrase that and say wrong to go to trial?" Only a couple of hands went up.

"Okay, business and economics majors, let's look at the math and then see. Can someone please tell me, what was our petitioner, James Paul McCartney's, opening offer?"

"Twenty million," a couple of the students said aloud simultaneously.

Another student pointed out that a year later, when there was still no settlement, Sir Paul McCartney offered his estranged wife five million pounds less in mediation, bringing his offer down to fifteen million pounds. So then I asked, "Before we analyze the case any further, could someone tell me what the court awarded her in the end? Sarah?"

She looked straight at me. "It was £24.3 million, Dr. Purdy."

"Thank you. Let's look at the case, people, because even by our most conservative estimate surrounding the numbers that went back and forth between the petitioner McCartney and the respondent Mills, our respondent will be exiting this marriage with £4.3 million more pounds than if she had agreed to settle out of court. So for those who think she was being greedy, what do you say now? Is it a waste? The numbers don't lie. Michael?"

"It's ridiculous. They were only married four years," he said. There was a pause, and I looked around the lecture hall to scan the expressions.

One student spoke out without raising her hand, "It's because they have a child." I decided to let my students debate this.

Then I could not resist commenting, "Well, Jennifer has a point. It's true if the child lives one lifestyle, you can't exactly have her mother living in a walk-up in Peckham—especially because I believe Justice Bennett does a good job of noting the burden of raising their daughter, Beatrice, will fall on whom, folks?" I paused. "After all, doesn't Justice Bennett point out that by the time Beatrice is about your age—twenty-two—her father will be how old? Yes, Kate."

"Old—he'll be eighty-three. I just want to say, I mean, maybe it's not that important, but I think he was kinda cheap with the nanny."

"Ah, yes, the nanny. Anyone else want to comment? I think Kate has an interesting observation. The majority of this case is overwhelmingly about Ms. Mills's postmarital needs, and we have only one paragraph of discussion of Beatrice's needs. Granted, it appears the McCartneys were able to work out most of the issues regarding their daughter without the court, but what about the nanny? Kate?"

51

"Doesn't the judge order him to pay the nanny more?"

Another hand flew up, so I called on him, "Ethan."

"Twenty-five thousand pounds a year for a nanny—I don't think that's cheap. I don't see why that had to go up. Why doesn't *she* pay for the nanny?"

When I heard that, I thought, *Well, they are young; they've never had children and or even been married.* I was very aware of the fact that I am the sole person in the lecture hall with marital experience.

Interestingly, this class showed that while none of my students have ever been married, they almost all have an opinion about Paul McCartney's second marriage. Practically the whole world had—or, better yet, still has—an opinion about the McCartneys' now terminated marriage. Unlike the rest of the world, however, my students have read the High Court's decision. They may not understand all of the legal terms—such as McKenzie friends, Duxbury fund, or Form E—but they understand the sum and substance of this case: divorce.

In fact, they are now so familiar that Ethan believes that—despite the fact Beatrice's musician father is worth, on a bad day, at least £400 million (about $700 million)—her currently unemployed, disabled, charitable campaigner mother should pay for her nanny. After Ethan's comment, I had to steer the class a bit into the unknown world (to them) of childcare.

"Ethan, do you think working for Sir Paul is a nine-to-five job? Do you think, when he goes on a concert tour, he is going to cancel his gig if it is his week with Beatrice and her nanny gets sick or the nanny's grandmother dies?"

"Probably not."

"Do you think he stops everything he is doing at seven o'clock at night because the nanny has to go home?"

"No."

"Do you think he never works weekends or goes out on a Saturday nights because Beatrice's nanny is unavailable?" My voice dropped, and I said, "Okay, gang, I admit I am revealing something about myself."

"No," Ethan replied.

"Do you think, given how famous he is, he can leave Beatrice with some random last-minute babysitter he finds on findmeababysitter.com?"

"No."

"Excellent, Ethan. Now, Beatrice may or may not be in full-time school at the age of four, but what time do you think she wakes up in the morning and what time does she go to sleep?"

At this point I had clearly stumped Ethan, judging from his expression. A couple of the young women in the class raised their hands.

"Sarah?"

"Well, I worked as a nanny last summer. I'd say she is up around seven every morning, and she probably goes to bed around eight every night—depends—maybe seven or seven thirty, if they are lucky."

"Thank you, Sarah. That sounds about right to me." I looked back at Ethan. "Ethan, you are a business major. How much money is Beatrice's nanny getting per hour?"

I paused while Ethan responded with a half-smile and a couple of his classmates actually started figuring it out on their phones.

"Ethan, have you taken research methods yet?" I decided to follow up with a question before he could answer. The class laughed. "I think you need to do some more research into the Central London nanny market before you can determine whether or not twenty-five thousand pounds a year is cheap."

I continued, "Why, Justice Bennett himself writes in the decision at paragraph two hundred forty-one, and I quote, 'Nannies are expensive; good nannies do not come cheap... Beatrice, a child of four with a father as wealthy as the husband... is entitled to a good nanny.'"

God bless Justice Bennett.

This is some of the most critical dicta to come out of this decision. After reading Justice Bennett's words, I had to resist saying aloud, "Amen, praise be the gospel by Lord Justice Bennett!"

The fact remains that most of us no longer have extended family living nearby. Even if we do, our parents are older and unable to keep up with our toddler children. Many parents in the West remain heavily, often desperately, reliant on babysitters to help them manage the rest of their lives.

We all need help in one way or the other, whether it is through a daycare center, friend, or nanny. To carry out such commonplace activities as going to the dentist, doctor, or hairdresser, people—nearly always women—need help with their children. I say women because I have observed in modern Western society it appears to be a man's birthright not to experience drastic disruptions to his daily life when he becomes a father. However, when a woman becomes a mother, a haircut is suddenly perceived not as routine grooming but as a luxury she can learn to live without. The fact that Justice Bennett recognizes in his decision that childcare is not cheap—and top childcare, such as a good nanny, is expensive—is, I believe, a huge leap forward for all parentkind. Too many people in this world view a nanny as a type of luxury comparable to an iPad or a designer handbag and not, in anyway, a possible necessity for contemporary families.

Some would ask why get a nanny when you can drop your child off in a crèche or day-care center? A day-care center is a room with seventeen other year-and-half-old children where your child gets little individual attention.

We know the growing brain needs individual attention to stimulate neurological development. A crèche or day-care center is not cheap, incidentally; it is, however, cheaper than a nanny, especially a good one. I acknowledge my standards may sometimes be high, but don't all children deserve the best start if they can obtain it? Do we, adult society, not owe them this minimum? I have discovered another thing in life I now know for sure: death, taxes, legal fees, and if Beatrice McCartney can't get a good nanny all the children of the world should be afraid—very, very afraid.

I think the decision is well written, but I want to know what my students believe. "What do you think of Justice Bennett's decision, Catherine?"

"Well, I don't understand why he brought her childhood into his decision."

"What do you mean, Catherine?"

"I mean how he writes Mills had a trouble childhood. Why does that matter?"

"Ah, yes, you mean paragraph eighteen, where he writes Mills had 'a rather troubled childhood.' Only a paragraph above, he describes McCartney as 'a world famous musician, composer, and singer... he is an icon to millions of people.' Well, Catherine has a great point. That jumped out at me as well when I first read the decision, if only for the reason I know no one on earth can be married to an icon; you marry a man, a human being. Trust me, Tiger Woods's wife, Elin, does not think her husband is an icon. Frankly, I'm surprised in a divorce proceeding any party would be referred to as an icon, even if it is to refer to the perception that others hold."

I wanted to get to the heart of the case. "So, business majors, two questions: One, why is Ms. Mills getting more money from the court? Two, on what does Justice Bennett base his final figure of £24.3 million? To help answer that question, Mills hires a forensic accountant. How many of you are taking accounting this semester with Dr. Michaels?"

About a third of the room's hands went up.

"McCartney's accountants and Mill's accountants disagree about the value of his business assets. But even by the most conservative estimates of his accounting team, which Justice Bennett decides to accept, Sir Paul McCartney's net worth is how much, gang? Sarah?"

"Four hundred million."

Another hand shot up. "Mary?"

"But doesn't she say he is worth eight hundred million pounds?"

"Yes, she claims he provided her that figure when they were together. Mind you, now they are divorcing, not dating, so the music has changed. Perhaps petitioner McCartney should have written a new song, a type of anthem that could be sung by many divorcing husbands: 'Baby, I am amazed I ain't got that kinda money.'" They laughed again, so I knew they were still really paying attention.

"Regardless of her claims we must go with what the judge decides, and he says it looks more like the four hundred million pounds. Okay, so money can't buy him love, but it will buy him auditors who can determine how much money he made during the course of this four-year marriage. The answer is… Mark?"

He fumbled through the pages of the case. His friend sitting next to him whispered the answer, so I decided to call on him instead, "Mohammed."

"I believe it was £39.6 million."

"Right. He makes a staggering £39.6 million during the marriage years. I say staggering for two reasons. The first is because of the amount, and the second—how was most of the money made? Patrick?"

"From his music?"

"Correct. It is mostly *passive* income due to royalties, growth in the value of his properties, et cetera. Simply by being Paul McCartney and letting the businesses he has in place run their course he made nearly forty million pounds, close to ten million a year." A hand shot up; he seemed eager. "Sam?"

"He did go on one tour, Dr. Purdy."

"Yeah," a student named Aysha added, "Where she gave him the idea to wear a fake nail while playing guitar."

"Ah, yes—the acrylic fingernail. Something they actually agreed upon was the nail was a great idea. Mills cites it as an example of her 'exceptional' contributions as a wife. I am quoting from the decision here in paragraph ninety-one, where she claimed to be 'his full-time wife, mother, lover, confidante, business partner, and psychologist.'"

For fun, I posed the question, "Well, gang, how much should you get for a fabulous fake nail idea? Keep in mind one of our litigants is a guitarist, so this fake nail is probably a bona fide tax-deductible business expense."

They got the joke, and I let that question sit for a moment. I started thinking how many women have had far better ideas for their husbands than how to prevent a blister yet get nothing. I wondered to myself, *What if Mills had suggested nail tips only, and it was McCartney who had figured out he needed an entire acrylic nail. Would it have reduced her settlement?*

"Thank you, Sam, for pointing out there was one tour. Okay, joking about the fake nail aside, let's get to the main question. How much is she getting percentagewise of what he made during the marriage? George?"

"Bit more than half."

"Correct, about sixty-one percent to be more precise. So, in reality, the court is awarding her a bit more than half of what was earned during the marriage. With this in mind, now what do you think of her settlement, Ethan?"

"Wait a second, Dr. Purdy, whose side are you on?"

"What do you mean side? I'm not on anyone's side. I am pointing out the facts. Frankly, after reading the decision, I'm happy I wasn't married to either one of them. Actually, in a funny way, I think they were perfect for each other. I mean, in paragraph ninety-six he says the acrylic nail idea was, I quote, 'brilliant.' Why, they sound very intellectually compatible—both vegetarians, yoga lovers—I am not sure why they got divorced." The class was smiling.

"By the way, this £24.3 million that the court awards Mills, is this, in fact, her final net figure?" I dropped my voice for a bit of fun and asked, "Is this the final answer?"

I wanted them to think about two issues here—some of their teacher's personal best definites in life—taxes and legal fees.

A pause. My audience looked a bit confused, so I rephrased the question. "Well, what is one of the first things Mills is probably going to do when she gets her money? Martin?"

"Doesn't she owe her lawyers money?"

"Good. People, let's not forget legal fees. This is essential to understanding litigation and the legal system. Is going to court cheap? Nina, you look confused."

"Isn't there a question about whether she owes her lawyers or if her lawyers owe her?"

"Yes, Nina has an excellent point. Mills disputed her final bill of one hundred seventeen thousand pounds from her solicitors, and the court says that bill is still being reviewed to determine whether she was overcharged. Okay, putting that final bill to the side, how much do we know she spent on legal fees? Nina?"

"A million, wait… actually a million three."

"Good, and how do we know this?"

"It's on her marked-up bank statements."

"Exactly. She claims she had two to three million pounds in the bank when she got married, but the court dismisses this claim of hers—why? Martin?"

"Because she has no proof. She couldn't come up with any papers to back it up."

"Correct. I like to point out Mills is unable to produce bank statements or tax returns to support her claim that she had two to three million pounds in the bank at the time she married. Justice Bennett writes in paragraph thirty that 'there is no documentary evidence to support that assertion.' He continues and states Mills was repeatedly asked to produce bank statements to verify this claim and that no banks statements have ever been produced to support this. This does not endear her to the court. She is, however, easily able to show the court bank statements that demonstrate she has spent a million pounds in legal fees to get unmarried. By the way, who is representing Mills in court now?"

They all answered, "She is."

"Right, she is representing herself and has a couple of friends with her that the court permitted her to bring, including her sister. Now, who is representing Sir Paul? Aysha?"

"Nicholas Mostyn"

"Correct, but read what it says on page one of the decision after his name."

"Nicholas Mostyn QC and Timothy Bishop instructed by Payne Hicks Beach Solicitors for the petitioner."

"Thank you. Can someone translate that for me? 'QC'—we've talked about that. What does this mean, Aysha?"

"Queen's Counsel."

"Good. QC stands for Queens Counsel—sounds terribly important, doesn't it? What do we know about QCs? Peter, hate to wake you back there, but what do we know about QCs?"

"Ah, yeah, QCs... huh... aren't they, like, really expensive?"

"That's right, and why are they so expensive? Sarah?"

"Because they are in the top ten percent of barristers."

"Good. What are the most common types of legal advocates here in the UK? Sarah?"

"Solicitors. You only need a barrister if you are going to court."

"Very good, gang. So we can see McCartney has hired two barristers, people to represent him at the courtroom bar. There is Mr. Mostyn, who is a QC, and his sidekick, the 'junior'"—I motioned quotes with both hands—"barrister, Mr. Bishop. Now, you may wonder why I put the word junior in quotes. He is a junior barrister. While *junior* is what he is called to distinguish him from a member of the Queen's Counsel, I want you all to realize Mr. Bishop is a highly experienced trial lawyer—especially if he is Mr. Mostyn's right-hand man. These barristers have years of courtroom experience and are arguably at the top of their game. Now, are McCartney's barristers his only lawyers?"

A few students looked at the decision to see if they could find other names and did not find anything. One student raised her hand. "Lena?"

"Well, wouldn't he have had a solicitor also?"

"Correct. Does everyone recall we discussed how barristers are usually hired or, as the decision says, instructed by solicitors? Here we see McCartney has hired the solicitors of Payne Hicks Beach—that's the name of the law firm from where he hired his solicitor, Fiona Shackleton. Shackleton's name is not in the decision, but she may be best known now for being the woman upon whom Mills dumped a glass of water when the trial finished. Shackleton was also the solicitor for the Prince of Wales when he divorced Princess Diana. So McCartney has three lawyers at court: two barristers, Mostyn and Bishop, and his solicitor, Shackleton. In addition, we can safely assume junior solicitors were involved at certain points organizing documents. We don't pay Mr. Mostyn to collate documents; that is a clerk's job. So what your teacher would love to know, but can't find out, is how much McCartney spent on legal fees. These people do not come cheap, gang," I emphasized, having personally discovered how true this statement was.

"By the way, how do lawyers do their billing generally? How much do you think top solicitors, such as Shackleton, charge for their time, business and economics majors? Alex?"

"I don't know, maybe two hundred pounds per hour."

"Any other thoughts?" I asked. I scanned the lecture hall during the pause. While no one had a hand up, they were all looking up and appeared genuinely curious. Ah, yes, lawyer's billing rates—one of the many things universities do not teach or discuss. Curiously, they are never part of the suggested curricula; however, it is impossible for a business student to become a flourishing business professional without knowledge of them.

"Nice try, my friend. More like five hundred pounds per hour at that time. Again, these are some of the most expensive lawyers in London.

Unlike McCartney, we do know how much respondent Mills spent on fees: a million pounds. By the way, do not feel too sorry for Mills not having a barrister, because she did have solicitors from the very prestigious law firm of Mischon de Reya representing her for probably about eighty-five percent of this case. Also, let's note we will probably never know if Mills fired her legal team or if they quit. Why might Mills have not had a barrister at court? Thomas?"

"I don't know, maybe sympathy?"

"Really? Well, I can safely say I don't think anyone would want to go up against Nicholas Mostyn without a barrister in an attempt to gain sympathy. That is just too much trouble."

Another student tried to answer so I called on her, "Yes, Shannon?"

"Yeah, and don't people get annoyed when someone represents himself? Like I've heard that they often don't know the procedures and how to do things the right way."

"Good point, Shannon. Yes, everyone in the courtroom starts thinking 'This is going to take forever because this bozo has a fool for a client' and 'We will be here all day while the litigant figures out how to respond.' The lawyers can get irritated, along with the judges and clerks, because they need to explain basic procedures to the *litigant in person*, as they say in the UK, or the *pro-se litigant*, as they say in the US. Any other thoughts as to why Mills may not have had a barrister at trial?"

Again, there was a pause so I posed the obvious question. "Marina, do you work for free?"

"No, not usually."

"Marina, let's say after taking my class you get so inspired you decide to study law. You later qualify and become a solicitor—we don't even have to get as ambitious as a barrister, with all that messy trial preparation. Do you think Mills would be your ideal client?"

"I don't know."

"Okay, well, putting any personal beliefs aside, who would you pick as your client: McCartney or Mills? Who do you think will be better able to pay their bills? Remember, it's not just paying the legal fees but also," I pinched my voice to say, "paying in a timely manner that is always appreciated." I continue in my regular voice, "Will it be the husband with a four hundred million pound net worth who wants to file for this divorce or the wife with no job, a minimal income of her own, and who goes on the morning news shows stating she became so depressed during this process she contemplated suicide?"

Marina nodded her head and smiled. Again, I refrained from saying the thought in my head that, although the media has been very tough on her, I still struggle to see how divorcing McCartney could cause Mills to become depressed. In fact, the more I study the decision, the better I understand how being married to McCartney could cause anyone to declare a need to have thirty thousand pounds worth of booze handy. This man, a father with a phenomenal net worth, had to be court ordered to pay the nanny more. I am starting to think Mills may be on to something here—perhaps *need* is too strong a word, but, better said, a new type of matrimonial *just compensation*. Sort of like *compulsory purchase*, when the government tells you it is going to pay you for your land because they are going to bulldoze through your house for that extra runway the airport needs. The government is required to provide just compensation, so why not a difficult ex?

I waited before speaking again and reflected on the plight of Mills. I could probably create a small nation of people who were, and remain, desperate to get away from their spouses but don't move for financial reasons. After all, the GP told me the other day I was the third person in his office that day complaining about this malady: living with the ex! Mills is getting out with millions of pounds and a gorgeous daughter to boot. This is a serious bonanza. Frankly, this woman should be celebrating every night for the rest of her life if you ask me, but I refrain from sharing this with my students. Of course, I can't help thinking I am fighting to keep the money from my own injury. Like so many women, I am fighting to keep what is mine, what I paid for, and for one roof to remain over my head. I am not Mills; I am not asking for several houses or money to maintain a wine cellar. Still, because she challenges our cultural expectations of what a wife is worth, this case fascinates me. No one questions why Beatrice, whose conception was clearly planned by both her parents as the case tells us, does not have her older father with £400 million take a hiatus from his career and stay home with her.

"Well, now that we know she spent over a million in fees, do you think she should have skipped going to court and settled in mediation? George?"

"No."

"No. Alright, why not?"

"Because she still made money."

"Right, even with the million she spent on legal fees, she still comes out at least three million pounds ahead."

A hand went up, so I called on the student.

"Yeah, but didn't she have to wait, like, almost two years?"

"Did everyone hear him? That is another very good point. Is going to court a speedy process?"

"No," they said.

"Aysha, let's say you find yourself going to court one day for some reason. The court assigns you a date, and you say that's a really bad day for you because you have something else planned. What do you think will happen if you say you can't make it on the day the court offers?"

"Um, I'm not sure, but I don't think you want to do that."

"Right. Do you think the next date the court can offer you is during the following week? Will the court clerk say, 'Oh sure, Ms. Nassir. Okay, how about the following Wednesday at ten o'clock?'"

"No."

"Correct. When do you guess the next available slot will be?"

"Alex?"

"Probably six months later."

"Sounds about right to me—maybe four or five months, if you are lucky. Now, one of the advantages to ADR that Lord Woolf and other UK government figures are always promoting is that ADR is faster and cheaper than going to court. There is a lot of truth to that statement, so why is anyone going to court? This ADR sounds fabulous. Chris?"

"There's no way to appeal a decision in ADR."

"Good. That is definitely one of the disadvantages. You usually can't appeal the decision given by a mediator or arbitrator. What else, gang?"

At that point I saw only a sea of empty faces.

"Let's learn a rule, people. Only a court has the power to force the production of documents or issue an injunction. Ever heard the words subpoena, summons, or witness order? That is a court order to produce testimony or evidence. When you go into some type of ADR, whether it is mediation or arbitration, a party can request documents but you are relying on the good will of the other to produce those documents—the good will and voluntary disclosure of a party with whom you are in a dispute. Sound a bit dodgy? If the McCartneys had mediated, Mills could not have gotten a forensic accounting of McCartney's business portfolio and the court would not have been able to see Mills could not produce documents to support her claim of having a net worth of two to three million pounds before getting married. This is one of the most vital differences between litigation and mediation. If you think someone is hiding something, never, ever agree to mediation."

I continued on. "Now, can someone tell me why we can read the *McCartney and Mills-McCartney* decision? Why was this published on the World Wide Web? Have the Royal Courts of Justice simply decided to engage in idle gossip?"

A few muttered no, but they did not raise their hands.

In response to their muttering, I asked, "Who paid for this? Who paid Justice Bennett for his time, business majors… Lisa?"

"Taxes."

"Correct—I did, people. Dr. Purdy is probably the only person in this room who is a UK taxpayer. I paid for the court's time. The public has paid for the courthouse, clerks, and judges, so I want to see—or at least read—the show. While matrimonial cases used to not be published in the UK, the government here has shifted to a more transparent style of publishing most decisions. Don't forget, the decisions are now law. If you can't settle your dispute outside of court and you need the government's resources, then know you have sacrificed your privacy." This was a lesson I was hoping to avoid learning firsthand.

"Now, don't get me wrong—mediation does have its place. For example, if two parties don't have any money, mediation is a far better choice than going to court. After all, zero from zero is what?"

A couple of students simultaneously said, "Zero."

"However, when a couple is divorcing, there is often a home—what then becomes known as the *matrimonial home*—or other assets involved. This is where things can get very tricky. Many would argue only getting your day in court, as the expression goes, would suffice to settle the matter fairly. The McCartneys are luckier than many couples regarding the division of their finances, because they are able to do what?"

Again, more silence, demonstrating their lack of marital experience, so I answered, "What can they do, with regard to their finances more specifically, that others can't do once they leave the courthouse, Lisa?"

"They can ask for a clean break."

"Correct. Whatever decision the court makes here will be what Mills is awarded. McCartney won't be paying her support, also known as maintenance or alimony. By the way, since we were speaking about taxes a moment ago, what is the tax status of Mills' settlement money?"

Tax is up there with legal fees—both are topics never covered enough with undergraduates.

A student said, "Yeah, I was wondering about that. Does she have to pay tax on this?"

They began to speak softly to themselves and almost automatically fell into little groups debating this question. I let them whisper for a few moments and listened to them ask one another. Then I answered, "No, the taxes have already been paid, so she gets it outright."

Curiously, most of the women had straight faces but a couple of the guys shook their heads. Then one of the guys said, "He should have had a prenup. Why didn't he have a prenup?"

"Good question. Why didn't Sir Paul have a prenuptial agreement? Does anyone know?" I suddenly realized the time and that we were out of it. "Because prenuptial agreements are not recognized in the UK. There is talk that may change but not yet."

I knew I was out of time but was compelled to address one student who had a nonplussed look on his face. "Mike, you seem baffled. What are you thinking?"

"I would have been happy to take a million and walk."

"Interesting. Well, a very different perspective than our respondent Mills. Mike, let's review the numbers and percentages. She gets £24.3 million. That is how much percentagewise of what was made during the marriage?"

"Sixty percent," a couple of the students said in unison.

"Good. Now tell me, how much is that percentagewise of McCartney's overall net worth?"

A pause then a hand. "Yes, Ally?"

"Six percent."

"Exactly, not many husbands can say their wife got only six percent of his net worth after their divorce. So, Doug, back to your original question as to why she needs thirty thousand pounds a year for wine—well, it looks like the answer is she is going to have to get it out of her £24.3 million."

With that I announced that during our next class we would move on to agency and partnership. There will be no need to bring Justice Bennett's decision to next week's lecture.

"You guys can leave the case at home—'Let It Be.'"

CHAPTER 4

Appropriate Behavior and Convenience Foods

28 March 2008 London

> Resentment is like drinking a poison and expecting the
> other person to die from it.
>
> —Malachy McCourt

I learned about resentment at the same time I learned about denial.
Resentment does nothing to the person, thing, or situation that is
resented. The subject of the resentment remains untouched, whereas the
resenter is attacked from within. Resentment is so powerful a poison
because it is insidious. Anger you can see—it's the loud voice, the door
slamming—but resentment hides so well. Initially, you keep refusing to
see it. Once you see it, you think you can control it. Finally, if you lie to
yourself about it long enough, the universe will force you to recognize it.
It hides in the body, like cancer. Also like cancer, something will come
crashing down to ensure you see it eventually. Resentment will hide for
ages, but once it decides it's time for recognition—it has the power to
shatter your world.

My state of denial blinded me. Slowly I began to recognize that I had
been disowning my feelings. I had foolishly thought I was successfully

swallowing, eating, and digesting my unhappiness. I failed to realize the more I ate, the more I was poisoning myself. My unclaimed emotion had become a pernicious dis-ease. It was a highly toxic tension.

I resented my confinement to home while Victor traveled the world in spite of our chronic shortage of money. Life alone with Thomas was challenging. Meeting Thomas's constant needs exhausted me. Your world shrinks when you are alone with a small child for twelve hours a day, four or five days a week. The earth mother herself would struggle. Still, I managed. I stopped exercising. I would visit with other mom friends during the day with young Thomas. I got my haircut or teeth cleaned on the occasional days I had a babysitter. I prayed the babysitters would not cancel, as it would mean another two months before I could get an appointment at the dentist. I went to bed when Thomas fell asleep. Sometimes I stayed awake for an extra hour to watch TV or call friends in New York. I never went out in the evening. When Victor returned home, he was too tired from his travels to want to go anywhere.

Then, when Thomas turned two and a half, I became really ambitious and wanted one more child. I knew Thomas would be starting school in September, once he turned three. What I didn't realize then was I could sacrifice two years of my life to be solely mother and nothing else but once I got to year three the resentment would take over. Still, trying for a second child reawakened our dormant sex life, albeit very briefly. However irrationally, I held out hope.

By the tenth week of the pregnancy I began experiencing the worst "morning sickness." It lasted all day and remained for the next several months. I lost weight. I struggled sometimes to even keep down water. Little Thomas would ask me to stop vomiting. "Mommy, please stop. I don't like it when you do that." Again, I needed someone to take care of me, but instead I had to take care of my darling, incredible two-year-old. Somehow I managed.

I did not want to recognize that I had become a *de facto* single mother. On the outside it appeared I was partnered, but my husband was seldom physically present. Even when he was home he was emotionally absent. Our marriage didn't even provide significant economic benefits. Whenever I asked him to put money into our joint account, he resisted. He hated taking money out of his business.

After Rex arrived, the marriage went from bad to worse. I was nursing him every two to three hours, never sleeping through the night. On top of that, I had to manage two-and-a-half-year-old Thomas.

Victor continued to build his business and travel. He would make some seemingly innocuous comment about not liking the food in business class on his flight, and all I could think was how wonderful it would be to have another human being serve me. How absolutely divine it would to eat my own food, off my own plate, without someone taking some of it or announcing he needed my help in the toilet or crying for me to breastfeed him immediately. I played the good wife, assuring him I understood. I had to suffer; money was tight, and we could not afford help.

Finally, as Rex approached his first birthday, I hired a babysitter so I could go out one evening. The next day, I spoke to Victor on the phone. I told him I had gone out to dinner with a friend. He asked with whom. Foolishly, I told the truth—with John, a mutual friend. Provocatively, Victor told me he thought I should have stayed at home. The conversation ended abruptly.

How dare my husband tell me not to go out when he spends so much time traveling the world? This time I was not swallowing my anger so easily. I looked at the clock and realized that two hours had passed. It was too late to call anyone here; it was, however, only seven o'clock in the evening in New York. I rang my old friend Jacqueline, hoping she would have left work by now and could speak freely. I told her about the conversation.

"Are you kidding? Hah, he's joking… right?"

"I wish. I mean, I stay home for three years breastfeeding his babies, looking like a cover girl for *National Geographic's Special Mammals Issue*, and he has the nerve to criticize me for this?"

"What exactly did he say?"

"He said he didn't think it was *'appropriate.'* I mean, Jackie this guy is an old friend, nothing more. Victor knows him."

"Your husband didn't think it was appropriate? Well, if he is so concerned with what's appropriate, maybe it's not *appropriate* that he is never home."

"I know. He does exactly whatever it is he needs to do, but meanwhile—back here at the ranch, where sleepless nights reign—he is nowhere to be found. He thinks he can leave me alone with his kids and then still have the right to tell me where to go and how to act."

Then I asked Jackie a question. I asked her because she works for a bank in New York; in fact, she works on a trading floor surrounded all day by men in finance—traders. It takes a special type of person to be a trader, a special breed of shark.

"Do you know any guys who don't do what they need to do? Who don't put themselves first?"

"Honey, not where I work. Sure, there are guys like that, but we don't know them. Did I tell you I ran into Silvio the other day?"

"Silvio, your ex? Didn't he get married a couple of years ago?"

"Yeah, he did. Would you believe I saw him in Vegas when I had that corporate getaway, team-building nonsense thing last month? Most of the guys on the desk wanted to go to Vegas. There was a smaller group of us who wanted the beach, including me, but we lost out to the Vegas crowd. Anyway, I saw Silvio in the casino. The only reason I was in the casino was because I don't play golf and I thought I better hang with my colleagues a bit. Grace, it was nearly two in the morning, and you should have seen the woman he was with—definitely a professional, a skank. I couldn't believe it. Talk about putting yourself first. He pretended he didn't see me, so I sent him a text that said, 'Is that your wife?'"

I loved the story because she'd made me laugh. I thought, *Well it's not just me who is having marital problems. Wonder if Silvio's wife is unhappy.* Then I asked Jackie if Silvio has kids.

"No, I don't think so. I would have heard through the grapevine."

I sighed, "Things are so simple when you don't have kids. What am I going to do, Jackie?"

"Let's be honest—nothing. The baby isn't even one yet. Even if you called me up in the morning and said you were leaving, I'd say no you are not."

"I just want to have a life again, but it's so hard with the boys and Victor's work. I don't understand why he is so difficult sometimes. I mean, I am busting my hump here, and he acts like all I ever do is complain."

"Look, Grace, you probably don't want to hear this, but I wouldn't be surprised if he is having an affair. He travels a lot—you would have no idea if he did."

"Jackie, I really don't think he is having an affair. Believe it or not, I could compete with another woman. The problem is I am competing with his career."

"Look, it's not my business anyway, but like I said, you are not going anywhere right now. Why don't you try sleeping through the night for a week straight before you take on anything else?"

We chatted awhile longer. She told me about some former classmates of ours she'd had lunch with the other day. It was a reminder of the life I once had: working hard outside the home; going out after work with friends; no mortgage or childcare responsibilities; promotions, pay increases, and recognition; focusing on yourself, your career, and some fun somewhere between it all.

After we hung up, I lay there in bed reflecting on what she'd said. Looking back at this phone conversation, I now see it was probably one of the first times I took a real step toward acknowledging my denied anger. I was exhausted and desperate for emotional support.

Jackie's comment about what was "appropriate" really hit me. Victor has said and done so many glaringly inappropriate things, which I've continually tolerated. I'll never forget when I went into labor with Rex. It was about six in the morning and my water had broken. I was nervous because with Thomas I had been induced, so I had never before experienced my water breaking. All I knew was when that happened, you go into high alert. I woke up Victor and said, "You've got to call me a taxi. We have to go to the hospital. My water has broken."

"Oh," he replied. "Do I have time to take a shower?"

I couldn't believe what I was hearing, but I was way too concerned about getting to the hospital quickly to get upset. I felt like offering him some of my water for a shower. All I said was, "Let's get something clear— today is not about you, Victor. Please call the taxi now."

I then swiftly moved to an inner dialogue with baby Rex, asking him to hang on until Mama got to the hospital. As I look back, I should have realized then we were doomed. Here I was about to give birth to his son and he was wondering if he had enough time to groom himself.

I did not reveal all my concerns to Jackie. When she suggested he was having an affair, I didn't tell her why I really believed he was not cheating. I was too embarrassed. I did not mention the strange charges I noticed on a credit card statement several months earlier that I'd had to investigate. When I tracked the charges, I discovered they'd bought him virtual pleasures.

Virtual woman are much better than real ones—they appear when it suits you and disappear when you are finished with them. All it takes is the click of a button. A real mistress is a human being who would inevitably make demands on him at some point. Again, I did my best to allow my denial to suppress my resentment; I let denial override my inner voice that said, *This is really bad, Grace. You can't be happy here.* While money was too tight for a babysitter, it wasn't too tight to pay for porn. I didn't even have the energy to fight Victor on that one. It was too depressing.

I experience Victor's marital presence mostly through the mode of his absence: the dry cleaning of his I collect, the laundry of his I wash, and the bills of his I pay—including his pornography. Thomas and I chat about him *in absentia*. He reminds me a bit of the mysterious "Charlie" in the '70s television show *Charlie's Angels*. Charlie is the man whom the Angels only experience through a speakerphone. At least our Charlie does have a brief cameo appearance on the weekends so the boys know what he looks like.

<u>30 March 2008 London</u>

> Children are educated by what the grown-up is and not by his talk.
>
> —Carl Jung

I'm at Phoebe's this Sunday, alone, while the boys stay at the flat with Victor. He hired a babysitter to come in for about four hours to help him with the meals. Victor has an allergy to cooking as well as public transport.

Being here alone has me thinking a lot about how different my parenthood experience has been from my parents. I could never have predicted how challenging parenthood would be based on my life as a child.

I was raised in New York by two working parents: my father, a lawyer who practiced as a courtroom litigator, and my mother, who worked for the State of New York. My father seldom traveled, while my mother rarely worked late because she worked for the State. In addition, there was a live-in housekeeper until I was about fourteen and no longer needed adult supervision.

For successful parenting, providing a degree of financial comfort may be necessary but that alone is not sufficient. Neither my mother nor father was the type to always put their children's needs first. My most vivid memory of our family living room was the enormous portrait of my mother that loomed large on the wall. A painting of her alone, not with the children; she was the queen bee, and no one was to forget that. It looked terrifyingly similar to the large portrait in the film *Mommie Dearest* that Joan Crawford hung of herself in her Hollywood living room. A few small Polaroid photos of my brother, Paul, and me were scattered throughout the living room, but nothing compared in size to the painting of my mother. The next largest image in the room was an eight-by-ten sepia-tinted framed photo of my father. Sometimes I wondered if my parents forgot what they looked like and that was why they needed their photos and portraits handy.

When the housekeeper had a day off, my parents bought "convenience foods"—the convenience they focused on was their own. We had frozen food, "TV dinners," or pasta. Another fake food we ate was something called SpaghettiOs; they came in a can. I am not sure what was in them, but I loved them and they made for an easy dinner.

Looking back, there was a lot of processed food, especially when I was a teenager. We ate and drank items with strange colors but even stranger names: Doritos, Pringles, Kool-Aid, Triscuits, Ring-a-Dings, Snickers, Fluff, and Pop Rocks. Sometimes we would stop in McDonald's for dinner. I would never serve my children most of the so-called "food" we ate in the late 1970s or 1980s, but it made my parents life a lot easier. In all fairness, it was the era—the height of the quick, easy, chemically processed meal. It made their lives easier.

They socialized a fair bit; this was a good thing. Though the housekeeper was off on the weekends, they always seemed to find a babysitter on the weekends when needed. Some of Paul and my favorites were the out-of-work actresses who would watch us. One in particular used to recite her lines for her next audition as we walked down the street. Paul and I adored the strange looks we'd get from people on the street as they watched us walk with a woman who appeared to be talking to herself quite loudly.

The best part of their socializing was that they threw parties. Paul and I always enjoyed their entertaining. They threw fundraisers for local politicians, Christmas parties, and sometimes dinner parties. Except for the dinner parties, my brother and I were always allowed to attend. We enjoyed talking to all of their friends. Their friends were interesting, hardworking New Yorkers, who worked across various industries—television, law, financial services—and they were kind to my brother and me. My parents always were at their most charming when guests came—probably another reason we liked their parties. They always hired the same bartender, a Jamaican fellow named Henry, to work at the parties. He was short man, fast to make a drink, funny, and he spoke with a very raspy voice. He seemed very assiduous. As I recall, his only shortcoming as far as my mother was concerned was that he could not make a salad. He was around for years. There always seemed to be help available when they entertained.

Victor had grown up in France and West Africa, Senegal, a place where help in the house is a given fact for professionals. His father was a diplomat working for the French government, so that's how they moved to Senegal. Nearly all of the non-Western cultures have lots of people help with children, either paid or unpaid—it's a way of life. They never raise their children like we do in the West, leaving the mother and newborn baby alone at home. They know it takes a village to raise a child; they don't need to be convinced. So my husband's parents always had a lot of help with their four children. Victor was the second child and the oldest boy. He has an older sister, a younger brother, and a younger sister. Through his family, my boys have lots of cousins. Once they left France, they had not only a housekeeper but a driver and a cook—not to mention a stay-at-home mother.

I see now that neither of our parents suffered or had to martyr themselves to be a parent. They were never unable to go out due to an inability to find someone to watch their children. They have no comprehension how much having a child can interfere with your ability to live the rest of your life. Victor's parents at least had a lot of help in the home. My parents would simply not acknowledge my or my brother's needs. I recall several summers asking to go to camp or do something, but to no avail. I recall imploring my mother to take me to the eye doctor, as I thought I needed glasses. She kept insisting there was nothing wrong. She did not want to be bothered with checking my vision. This was inconvenient. Sure enough, once she finally relented, the doctor confirmed I was correct. I had to grow up quickly in that house. I had to parent myself a lot. Consequently, I became determined not to be self-centered with my children.

My parents were narcissists; it wasn't simple ignorance. My father met my mother when he and a friend bought the small modeling agency my mother was signed to early in her modeling career. My father literally bought himself a pretty future wife. I once asked him why he bought the agency. He replied that he and his friend "thought it would be fun." My father would never have the courage to say, "Because I wanted to fuck a model."

As my mother's modeling career advanced, she moved to the newly formed Wilhelmina Models, a top agency that discovered supermodels like Iman. Wilhelmina Cooper, a Dutch-born model, bravely decided to start her own agency. This was noteworthy, as this was still in the days where the agency got all the money and the models got little—decades before the days a model like Linda Evangelista would announce she "did not get out of bed for less than $10,000 a day."

Wilhelmina Models, however, was the start of the shift. Wilhelmina was maternal and very protective of her models. It was the late 1960s, and these women were known in New York as "Willy's Girls." I think being one of Willy's Girls may have been the closest my mother ever got to feeling like part of a happy family. Unlike many models, my mother did successfully switch careers when she went to work for the State a few years later. Still, I'm not sure she ever recovered from missing her carefree youthful days as one of Willy's beautiful flock of lambs.

My mother was obsessed with her physical appearance. Her self-esteem, the little she had, was based on her looks. Over the years, this left her repeatedly embittered and her joy in life limited. Having a thin teenage daughter did not help her. My father never paid much attention to what was actually happening in the house. He was happy to have a stunning-looking wife to sleep with and who appeared to the outside world to be functioning.

"Just don't get fat. Woman look horrible when they get fat." This was something I recall my father saying often. He would have noticed if my mother got fat. Fortunately, the universe made me a naturally thin woman, so I avoided developing an eating disorder.

I'll never forget the day my mother came home a blonde. (Her natural hair color was dark brown.) I was sixteen. I walked into the living room one evening to take a break from my homework to find my mother asking my father if he noticed anything new. My father replied, "New dress?"

I'll never forget where I was standing and the speech balloon in my head, *Jesus, we are all going to pay for that one, Dad.*

I tried to reassure my mother that her hair looked great. Sure enough, my mother filed for divorce several months later. I can't blame her; she was married to a man who couldn't notice her hair color but would notice if she gained ten pounds.

My brother and I were always aware of our mother's pain, and we stepped around it. We lived in an emotional minefield and learned to put the emotional needs of our parents above our own. My mother would return home from work every night to lie down alone in her room and watch TV, complaining she was tired. She never ate with my brother or me during the week, even if she was in the apartment. Her mood was usually foul, and we never wanted to aggravate it.

Their self-centeredness left both my parents unable to really see either my brother or me. They were always concerned with their own needs instead of their children's. My parents entrusted the help in the house with attending to us. Occasionally, something would happen that they had to address, like me needing eyeglasses or the help screwing up so much they had to acknowledge it. A classic example I recall is my mother explaining to our apartment neighbor why she'd finally fired one of the live-in housekeepers. "Well, I had to let her go after the second time I caught her putting MSG in the food."

Finally, after catching the maid putting a known carcinogenic in our food more than once, my mother decided she would have to look for new help. Mind you, at least she discovered the poisioning. My father would never have noticed any of it. That's why my brother and I liked our parents' entertaining and parties. It was one of the few times they paid warm attention to us—when others were watching and they could promote their self-image as concerned parents.

As a child, my parents confused me. As an adult, I realize their narcissistic behavior was probably part of a severe personality disorder. The disorder inflicts deep wounds on the family members of narcissists. One result of my parents' psychic disability was that I became hell-bent on never, ever being like that with my own children. The problem was all I knew was pain, and so I married a man I believed to be emotionally muted. It was familiar to me.

When it came to the boys, people told me I could do things differently. The main thing everyone kept telling me was to not breastfeed. "Stop nursing at three months," they all said. "You don't have any help, you don't have any family nearby, and your husband is not home." While it was obvious to outsiders that I should stop breastfeeding, it was not an option to me. Ironically, what my friends did not realize is when you are alone it can be easier to nurse. No bottles to sterilize, no formula to measure. Most women bottle feed in order to enable someone else to feed their child, so they can get a break. Not true for me—bottles just gave me one more thing I had to clean. I was already exhausted enough;

the last thing I wanted was another domestic chore. I was consumed enough by the laundry between feeds.

Finally, it all started to bother me. People were trying to give me suggestions on how to make my life easier, but all I heard them suggest was ways to cut corners raising my children. Perhaps I am too much of an academic, but I looked at the research surrounding breastfeeding versus bottle-feeding and it is astonishing. We know babies are better off if breastfed. Breastfed babies have higher IQs, lower rates of obesity, and better functioning immune systems. Mother Nature designed the mother–child relationship so that a mom can't be separated from her child for more than three hours the first several months of the baby human mammal's life. If you have ever nursed a child, you know that feeling when you think your breasts are about to explode because you need to release the milk in them. Your body tells you it is time to reconnect physically with your infant. He or she needs Mama—now. There is no busier human being on earth than a nursing mother. It provides a whole new definition to the idea of being "tied up" or "in a meeting."

I breastfed both boys on demand for a year. Consequently, I didn't sleep through the night for the first year of either of my two sons' lives. Through all this I ran the home: I cooked, cleaned, paid all the household bills, and organized playdates. I shopped for groceries, children's clothing, toys, and Christmas trees. Why, I even went back to work part time when my second son was just under a year old. I was hell-bent on being a superwoman, and my husband could not bother to eat a meal with me, let alone cook one. I was his servant, but one who had access to his checking account. After all, he was way too busy to bother with anything as trivial as paying household bills.

Sometimes I tried to convince myself that doing something as routine as going to the supermarket by myself was a luxury. It was not enough. Mind you, I suspect many marriages are like this to some degree and the parties continue on for one reason or another. I, however, was painfully reminded of how short life is once I fell ill. Then again, lots of women suffer and martyr themselves to be a better mother—but I am not sure that helps anyone in the end.

I never wanted my children to feel the pain I'd suffered from having such self-involved, emotionally absent parents. I wanted to avoid becoming narcissistic like my parents. I devoted myself so wholly to being the perfect mother and wife, the resentment ate at my body until I broke. My life was all about meeting other's needs.

The Victor I thought I loved probably never existed. The handsome, smart man I married provided an opportunity to erase the past and to live far away from what was familiar.

People comment on how brave I was to move to Spain or France, but I know the truth. I was wandering some of the greatest cities on earth looking for a home. After all, what's not to like about Madrid or Paris or London? The truth is it is so easy to leave a dysfunctional family behind. As an adolescent, I counted the days until I could find some excuse to grab my passport and fly away—to anywhere but here. I can learn French.

Pourquoi pas?

CHAPTER 5

Are You Sure You Want to Do This?

2 April 2008 London

> It may be true that the law cannot make a man love me, but it can keep him from lynching me, and I think that's pretty important.
>
> —Dr. Martin Luther King Jr.

The meeting with Sandra was difficult, but completing the marriage timeline and hearing the whole story from start to finish did give me a strange sense of clarity. The calm, however, did not last long. Yesterday Sandra called to say Anne would like me to come down to the office this week for a short meeting. Aside from a review of the timeline, there were a couple of outstanding matters that needed to be addressed—would tomorrow suit? "Yes, I can come in the morning before lecturing in the afternoon," I said. It needed to be late morning, once the boys have left for school/nursery.

Sandra met me in reception. She made polite conversation—asking how I was doing, how was the weekend—and then we went back to the same conference room where we'd worked the other day. There she handed me a piece of yellow paper.

"So we have received some answers to the nationality question. Why don't you read this fax?"

The fax was on a piece of bright yellow paper clearly designed to stand out. From the names and addresses on top of the letterhead, I could see it was from a French law firm. It was addressed to Anne, and it read:

> I understand your client's husband has French citizenship and that your client has a French passport; they both currently live in London. Considering the European nationality and residence of the parties, the jurisdiction of the divorce will be ruled by the European regulation 2201/2203…

After citing pieces of the European regulation it continues:

> Most likely, your client has French nationality and her husband could petition for divorce in France. In my opinion, and if your client does not have the same level of income as her husband, it would be much more interesting for your client to issue a divorce petition in England, as the first court to which this has been referred to would be competent for the entire divorce case.

I looked up at Sandra. "So this is saying that he could file for divorce in France since we both have French nationality, albeit as naturalized citizens."

"Correct." Sandra had a serious look on her face. Sandra then explained the regulation the fax is quoting is from the Brussels II treaty. Under this treaty, the first European court to be approached for a divorce decides it. I realized Dr. Purdy was about to get a lecture on European Union (EU) treaties. Brussels II is a EU regulation designed to prevent people of different European nationalities spending forever fighting in different European courts as to which EU country oversees a couple's divorce. Lawyers have a fancy expression for this: "forum shopping," meaning skipping around to find the place that is most favorable for you to sue. Laws differ from place to place, or jurisdictions, as the law calls it. I realize, though I have not yet served my divorce petition, my own life has become, in fact, a fabulous exam question. It is too advanced a question for my undergraduate business students, but it is a great question for family law students:

> Facts: H is French, W is American. W acquired French nationality during the course of her marriage to H. (She is a dual national.) H&W were married in New York but have resided in England almost all of the marriage.

> Exam Question: In which country or countries can they seek a divorce?

Sandra explained that the English courts are traditionally kinder to the nonworking or lower-income-earning spouses, like me, than French courts. The sooner I file my divorce petition, the better. I am in need of the English court's equity—a term I often explain to my students. *Equity:* that which is *equitable* or fair.

"You see," Sandra said, "they write it would be better for your client to file in England."

I looked back down at the fax, "I notice their exact words, that it would be 'more interesting' for me to file here—so French."

I lived in France briefly when my husband and I were first married, and I know that "interesting" is a critical word for the French. A French lawyer would never say "she better get her ass to the English High Court now," only that English law is more *"interesting."* I know with the French, you don't dare get bored. Why, the French prefer having a president who, while in office, gets divorced and then quickly remarries—provided it is to someone "interesting"—rather than have a boring leader. Carla Bruni-Sarkozy, the French president's wife, is a former supermodel turned singer. She is someone who left Eric Clapton to become Mick Jagger's mistress while he was married to Jerry Hall. Now she is interesting—beautiful and interesting. *C'est parfait.*

Contrast Madame Bruni-Sarkozy with Lionel Jospin, the boring French Socialist politician who ran for president against Jacques Chirac. Jospin's supporters tried to help make him more "interesting" by putting him in pink ties and getting him to blame his failure to take medications as the reason he made foolish remarks about President Chirac's age. It didn't work. Monsieur Jospin was and is smart, an intellectual, former professor, and corruption free but, alas, boring. He got fewer votes than the French equivalent of the head of the Nazi Party. After the election, Monsieur Jospin wisely conceited defeat. The French were very happy never to hear much from him again (more or less).

The French love to speak in a manner that, on the surface, avoids possible conflict. It doesn't matter if they are speaking in French or English; there are always codes, and it takes time to learn them. Hearing the French lawyers suggest it would be more "interesting" for me triggers my memory of a former Parisian boss whom Victor described to junior colleagues as a "quiet achiever." Again, to really speak French, a native English speaker must be able to recognize the code. A French "quiet achiever" is what Americans would call an obsequious waste of space, an anti-rainmaker, a nonproducing guy who in a good year, perhaps, can create one solid storm and hope it carries him for the next three. He is a man who is only a few steps above Willy Loman, Arthur Miller's salesman in *Death of a Salesman*. This type of businessman can exist more comfortably in France, because the right connections will carry you further than in the United States. Remember, though, the French "quiet achiever" is also the nonconfrontational term for someone who is not "interesting." His time is limited in both cultures; he just gets a bit more time in France.

Anyway, I know I am not *interested* in reading my husband's legal papers in French. Filing in England is the first piece of critical advice I have received from my lawyers.

Just as I finished reading the fax, the conference room door opened and Anne entered. After saying hello, she explained she was tied up in court the other day and, therefore, unable to address the nationality issue earlier. Anne looks as one would expect an English solicitor to look: fair skinned; well-spoken; with shoulder-length auburn hair; about my height, at five feet six; and often, but not always, wearing tweed. She is, as always, dressed in a smart skirt suit and very focused on the matter at hand.

"I see you have the fax regarding the nationality issue." Her eyes were looking at the yellow document in front of me.

"Yes, Sandra gave it to me a couple of minutes ago."

"Grace, you need to serve Victor now. French courts are very paternalistic. You don't want this divorce being heard in a French court. As you know, I've always been concerned that you held French nationality, despite having lived here in England."

"And simply filing the petition in the court is not enough?"

"Correct. We need to lodge the petition and then serve him personally. Sometimes you can do it by post, but I don't advise that given the circumstances. Given the urgency of getting the matter into an English court, personal service is needed so we have his acknowledgment of service automatically."

"Okay, I get it. This certainly adds a sense of urgency." I looked out the window, took a deep breath, and sighed. I then looked over at both Anne and Sandra. "He travels so often. I guess we just have to work around that as best we can?"

Anne responded with her usual calm, controlled voice, "Yes, we have managed to serve people who travel. We will have to talk about where you think it is best to serve him."

I haven't worked with Anne long, but one of the things I appreciate is no matter what I see as a challenge I can tell it is all simply another day's work for her. The way she responds in a calm, controlled voice, I know she has seen far worse in her years of practice.

"Also, while we are all here, I want you to know I have contacted a barrister regarding your critical illness insurance money."

The critical illness insurance money is the other part of this divorce that makes it complicated. Before I met Anne, I suspected my insurance money would make this divorce more unusual. After meeting with her, she told me there were two issues she needed to research further: our nationalities and this insurance money. While life insurance has been around a long time, critical illness insurance is a relatively new insurance product. It is commonplace nowadays for banks in England to offer both life insurance and critical illness insurance to anyone in England applying for a mortgage. When we took out a mortgage, we took out a critical illness policy on both of us as part of the standard procedure. What wasn't commonplace is the second critical illness policy I took out. I took this policy when my husband decided to launch his own financial advisory business. We looked at policies for both health and life when he decided to become self-employed. This second policy is the one that is now funding my legal fees. I was happy Anne had been able to do research on the status of it. What I am unhappy about it is what she told me next.

"It's not certain that it would be all yours, despite the illness being personal to you. That is the other reason why I wanted to meet with you today. I have spoken with the barrister I'd suggested, Robin Sharp, and she has agreed to represent you if you wish. Given the complications of the case and the fact that you can't afford a QC, I strongly recommend her as our best bet."

Things are getting more complicated daily. It seemed only the other day I was mustering up the courage to meet a lawyer, and now I have been advised I urgently need to file my divorce petition. In addition, I need a barrister. I trust Anne when she says I need a barrister, but I know that won't be cheap. These past couple of weeks I feel like my life has been moving faster than the speed of sound.

In England, you need to meet with a barrister for one reason only—you are going to court. This will become the irony of my situation: I am the "nonworking spouse" who, due to illness and insurance proceeds, will contribute over half a million pounds in cash to the marriage. I looked at both Sandra and Anne.

"Anne, it was a lot of money. He can't claim I didn't contribute. I still find it a bit rich that I am in the position of being the 'nonworking spouse' given how hard I worked while he traveled and how much money was contributed via the insurance. He has profited from my illness. For God's sake, when the bank called me I elected to pay off the mortgage! I should have taken the cash. I had that option with the bank, to take cash and not pay off the mortgage. Then I allowed him to convince me to take another mortgage so we would not drain his business! Now we still have a mortgage on the damn flat, and you are telling me it isn't clear if that money is mine?" I heard the tone of my voice and the sound of self-loathing. I am accepting I need a barrister and know she won't be cheap. Just as I said aloud, "I should have taken the cash," I realized I could have used that cash to pay my now-mandatory barrister.

"Grace, you can't do that. You can't go back and put yourself in the position you are in today back then," Anne said. "I always tell my clients this. It doesn't work. Please trust me. I have seen that too often over the years. We have talked about the insurance money, and we will need to instruct a barrister on this. It does make things more complicated."

"Okay... I guess you are right."

In fact, I suspect telling me I need to file now and, secondly, that we can't look back on yesterday from where we are today are two of the best pieces of advice I may get through this process. I console myself that at least with the second, smaller critical illness policy I got smart; I took that money and hired lawyers to get out of this marriage.

This process has gone from a snowball to an avalanche down the mountain, and I can't stop it even if I wanted. Sandra explained a bit more about the steps going forward. She then collected her papers and put them all back in a file. Then, before all three of us got up from the table, she paused, looked me right in the eye, and asked, "Are you sure you want to do this?"

"You know, Sandra, when I said to Victor I was disappointed we had to take out another mortgage after paying off the first one, I'll never forget his reply, 'Such is life.' That is when I said to myself, 'No, Victor. Such is life with you.'"

I paused took a deep breath and said, "Yes, I'm sure."

I am sure. While it has taken me a long time to come to this decision, I know it is the right one. Working with Sandra and providing the details of the marriage has enabled me to see the invisible dangers that reside in our union. One of the reasons I am certain I want to end this marriage is because I know now my husband, Victor, is a man whose emotional needs are met by his work and not anything a woman could give.

Married life has taught me that when work meets a person's emotional needs, another mere mortal can never compete. Work never provides emotional conflict; in fact, it is a bottomless well that continuously provides for those that feed at its trough. People love to marry money, but when a person marries you when they are already married to money—you really feel a fool.

People talk all the time about people who marry *"for* the money." Curiously, they seldom talk about people who can *only* marry money. Seldom do we hear gossip about the men and women who pretend they can marry another human being when all they can really commit to is their work and the recognition and money it brings. It may be because Western society so falsely values people who can make money and "be successful." I think those who can only marry money are far worse than people who allegedly marry a person because he or she is financially rich. At least with a gold digging fortune hunter you can see his or her hand. Trust me, even if one of the spouses can't see it, the couple's friends have seen it for years. "Well, we all knew she/he was only after his/her money."

But when someone is married to money through his or her work, you never know exactly where you stand. You can try to compete for attention, but work is really what interests him or her. Work is the old friend that never leaves or makes foolish demands. Curiously, it doesn't matter how much actual money people like that have or earn because, regardless, it is never enough. The more money they make, the greater the recognition and the better the high. People married to money give it all their energy and have nothing left for others. They are deceptive; they are usually master manipulators who label their work "stressful" and expect you to feel sorry for them because they have been under their own self-imposed pressure and have nothing left to give.

They refuse to acknowledge they are like drug addicts who keep getting high or alcoholics who keeps drinking. Because their drug of choice—work—is not illegal, you are supposed to pity them and not be upset you haven't gotten a need of yours met in months. They will tell you they are too tired for sex and yet have the audacity to pour a drink and eat right in front of you. You never see them too tired to drink or eat. They always have energy for their clients, work, and colleagues. They become almost subhuman, engaging only their most basic needs and suppressing all others so they can devote more time to working. Their existence is primarily all about the next fix—their next professional success. Spouses and friends almost always fall on the list of "things that can wait."

I know I need to get divorced.

24 April 2008 London

> A true friend never gets in your way, unless you happen
> to be going down.
> —Arnold H. Glasgow

While I did not plan for events to unfold as they did in the days leading up to the weekend in Madrid, I have come to the conclusion that everyone needs friends when they are getting a divorce. It is especially handy to have friends who happen to live in Spain. Even the North Pole might be nice; good place to get away.

The sense of relief I gained from actually serving Victor has been short-lived. He had not anticipated finding a divorce petition at work and was unhappy because, suddenly, I had interrupted his plans. He had planned to be traveling all week but now had to interrupt his schedule to find a solicitor. I discovered this on Monday morning when we all awoke in the flat.

I had crept back into the flat late on Sunday night and went straight to sleep, alone in my room while Victor slept in Thomas' room. I'd tried to phone over the weekend and got only his voicemail. I left an apology message. I wasn't surprised he would not take my call. On Monday morning, while attending to the boys, we spoke very briefly. Victor was cold and curt, as is his usual custom. He got up to go to work as usual and, again, I said I was sorry.

His only response was, "Yeah, so am I. I was supposed to be going to Johannesburg today. Now I've had to postpone my trip to meet with my solicitor!"

Curiously, he did not seem terribly disappointed that I had asked to terminate the marriage; he mentioned to me only his unhappiness at not being able to be with his client on Monday. The separation from his client seemed to make him unhappier than the end of his marriage. For once he had to factor me in, and I was, perversely, delighted. By filing for divorce, I managed to get on his calendar—and I knew this time he would not cancel. I knew he would answer me, because if he did not the court would quickly grant me the divorce without his input.

Why, this time I even knew *when* I would get the answer. Under English law, he had ten days to respond. It was fabulous. When he responded, my mind drifted to thinking about how many marriages could be saved if every time a husband ignored a wife she could file an "answer petition" with the courts: Husband has eight days to respond. Failing to respond is a default answer in favor of wife; wife can then make all decisions. Filing a divorce petition means your husband won't ignore you, cancel, reschedule, postpone, or sit on his smartphone while "listening." Unless his Blackberry knows the rules of English family law court procedures, he will have to respond. Perhaps he could switch his Blackberry to an iPhone and see if Apple has an app for divorce proceeding responses. Or, if that is too technical, maybe they have other helpful apps, such as "good divorce lawyers" for the different countries where they distribute their phones. That way their customers could at least start the proceedings without ever having to put down their phone. "Damn, my wife served me a divorce petition. Do you have an app for that?"

Since Madrid, things have become increasingly strained. I now stay at Phoebe's house when he is home on the weekends. In fact, if it weren't for Phoebe, I'm not sure how I would be getting through the process.

I met Phoebe a few years ago, when I first arrived in London, through some mutual acquaintances. We quickly became friends. She is a transplanted Californian who married an Englishman, and that's why she moved here. Sporty, blonde, and smart, she soon became a great friend and resource about information regarding life in London.

Before breast cancer or my divorce, it was Phoebe who gave me the idea to enter academic life. She is a psychologist with a doctorate from the University of California, Los Angeles, who went straight into academics after completing her degrees. She was a full-time academic in both the United States and, later, the United Kingdom. More recently, she's been working part-time since her first child was born.

One day, when I was pregnant with my second son, I was lamenting to her about how much I missed my professional life. We had met for coffee right after she'd finished a lecture. Working for a living, let alone doing something as demanding as practicing law, would have been impossible given the chronic nausea I had to endure. Even though the nausea was finally improving, I think I had already decided this would be my last pregnancy.

I remember telling Phoebe that I had recently inquired into taking the qualified lawyers test so I could practice in England. The problem was Victor traveled abroad too often. In addition, I had no family around to help. I couldn't see how I could manage the soon-to-be two kids while working the demanding hours the practice of law requires.

"Have you ever thought about teaching?" Phoebe asked me.

"No, what do you mean?"

"I mean lecturing. Didn't you tell me you used to do a lot of management training when you were at the insurance company?"

"Yes, I did run a lot of courses around the US about company employment practices—you know, don't say illegal, offensive, or foolish things when you fire someone. I am not sure that is the same as teaching."

Phoebe looked at me and said, "Sounds like a lecture to me. Really, you should think about it. I think you have the right personality for it, Grace."

She continued, saying, "Law is not my department—psychology is always in the sciences—but I could forward your CV to my department head, Chris. We have to work on your CV to make it more academic, but I really think you should consider it."

Phoebe's encouragement into academia has proven to be much more valuable than I could have imagined at the time over coffee. Fortunately for Phoebe, she has not been the only one who has provided me with support over these challenging months. My other pal, Liz, has too. All three of us are Americans who married Europeans and settled in Europe. They know what it is like to try to raise a family without any family nearby to help. They both tell me they can't imagine how difficult it would be to get a divorce under these circumstances. Everyone who is getting divorced needs a couple of friends nearby upon whom she or he can rely.

CHAPTER 6

Crazy Kuwaitis and Typhoid Maria

29 April 2008 London

> Neither shall you allege the example of the many as an excuse for doing wrong.
>
> —Exodus 23:2 NAB

As the tension mounts in the flat at home, I realize that my lecturing work and staying at Phoebe's place on the weekends are my primary escapes for the strain in my personal life. Phoebe usually goes away to the countryside with her husband and kids on the weekends, and so she kindly offered me her place when they are gone. Granted, Victor and I do a good job of not of arguing when he returns, but still, I can't feel at home in my own home. Yesterday, I found myself explaining, or should I say spilling it all out, to Phoebe.

"I am probably going to have to sell. He won't move. I am starting to think we will be legally divorced and still living in the flat together. It's the only way to end this 'put up or shut up' hell I am in. I can't go on living this way—my flat during the week, his on the weekends while I go to yours."

Phoebe interjected, "Okay, listen, I know the flat isn't big, but it's not small either, and you are in a great part of London—why, it's one of the best parts of Kensington."

Kensington is the neighborhood—more precisely, the borough—where Phoebe and I both live. It is sometimes referred to as "K&C," a shortened version of the longer name, The Royal Borough of Kensington and Chelsea. A neighborhood with almost no high-rises, loads of green communal garden squares, and where at half past eight on any given weekday morning the streets are littered with schoolchildren wearing the required jacket, tie, and hats of their school uniforms. (The English always require school children to wear formal uniforms, whether in a fee-paying or state school.) A place universally considered upmarket.

"I know, and I also know I need to hear that—thanks. It's just the thought of moving, along with everything else. But, as Liz reminded me the other day, the purpose of all of this is to get on with my life. Besides, if I don't sell I'll be living in a property he half owns; that won't work. Still, I would have cracked by now if you guys had not lent me your place on the weekends. I think the cats are getting used to me."

"Don't mention it. Really, it's good for us to have someone there when we are away. Hey, how's the new class going?"

Phoebe was a pal; she had told Chris, her department head at the university, to find me another class. "Chris, she's getting a divorce, and she needs the work."

A class did manifest itself. While it is more adjunct/part-time work, so the pay is low, it is a new class and I can do what I want with it. I needed the class for a couple of reasons: Firstly, I needed to expand my repertoire of classes. Secondly, work is probably going to be one of the best pieces of therapy to help me through the divorce process. Professing leaves no room for distractions, no desk to hide behind, no obsequious colleagues adjacent to you who are delighted to do all the talking—it's you and you alone, so get on with it. That is how I found the new class Phoebe is referring to, Introduction to Business.

"Well, frankly, my dear, lecturing to freshmen has been an experience for me. They just don't have the maturity of upperclassmen. I mean, you can just see who is not going to make it to graduation."

"I hated teaching freshmen. I remember one semester Chris begged me to teach Intro to Psych. I had nearly one hundred students—can you imagine one hundred freshmen and all their nonsense? 'Do you have any more handouts?' Of course, this is after they missed class. Then they give you their crap reasons for why they missed class. Do I care that they missed class? Hey, that student you mentioned the other day—he hasn't come back, right?"

That student that Phoebe was referring to is some kid from the Middle East who freaked out, throwing a cup of coffee on the ground at my feet, when he was unhappy with his midterm grade. This was after he stood up in the middle of lecture, approached me at the front, and handed me a note. The note wasn't very coherent, although it did say something about the fact he drove an expensive car. He then left the lecture hall to wait for me outside, where I saw him after class. Fortunately, a bunch of other students were around to witness his rant. After he'd finished with his outburst, one of his classmates came up to me and said, "He is crazy."

The witnessing student even offered to let the university know what he had seen. I thanked him and said that would not be necessary. I immediately left campus. All I could think was, *You have got to be joking. I am not plugging into this. I am already living with someone I am suing, I'll be damned if I come to work to deal with some nut job—a student nonetheless, not even an administrator. If I wanted to do that, I'd apply for the job of dean of student shit, I mean, dean of student life.*

"The crazy Kuwaiti? No, he's gone. Apparently, he was driving like a madman the other day with some other students in the car, and they said something to the powers that be. Anyway, the rumor is he has been partying too much and is en route back to Kuwait. Did I tell you he had the audacity to freak out for getting a B when it turns out his grade point average is about a 2.00? Not to mention his excessive absences."

"God, Grace you really don't need that. Did you tell your department head like I said you should?"

"Yes, reluctantly. You know, I just didn't want any more drama. Also, do you remember Reza, the economics lecturer? Well, they just made him the acting department head because of John's departure. Honestly, Reza couldn't manage a two-car funeral, let alone the faculty. Everyone in the Business Department is complaining."

"Yeah, I had heard about his appointment and was pretty surprised," Phoebe said. "I know you don't need the drama, but you had to tell the university about him. What did the department do?"

"Reza and I had a meeting with the head of human resources. They agreed to put me in a classroom with a CCTV camera if he returns. After the meeting, I told a colleague of mine what happened. She told me there are rumors that this student bribes faculty. I have no idea if the rumors are true, but I couldn't figure out why he was so angry or why he thought I'd give a damn about his car. Then it dawned on me—he knew he was going to have to work in my class. He probably thought "that bitchy American woman won't take money" and realized he was going to have to actually *study* for my exam. I don't take bribes. You'd think he would be grateful for the B, given the rest of his grades! I checked them out on the system. I swear, no good deed goes unpunished. Integrity isn't cheap—boy, have I learned that this year."

"So true. Anyway, the semester has only a few more weeks, and then you will be in New York with the boys."

"I know, and I can't wait. Anne was reminding me of that at a meeting the other day. I told her the living situation is really getting to me, but she reminded me I would be away soon. I don't think I'll be back until mid-August—did I tell you that?"

"No," Phoebe said, "but I figured you'd stay away as long as possible. Hey, I am not trying to pressure you, but have you started looking at apartments, even just on the web? I think you should start looking just to get a feel for what's out there."

"Not yet, but I know you are right. Probably after I get back from New York. Would you believe I am actually looking forward to marking finals—only because that means I am that much closer to getting out of here for the summer?"

I refrained from telling Phoebe that in the past few months, Introduction to Business has introduced me to other sundry students, aside from the crazy Kuwaiti. During the third week, a student who had not previously attended arrived and approached me after class. Her name was Maria, and she said she had been unable to attend sooner because she had been sick.

"Hi, I am really sorry I wasn't here the last couple of weeks, but I was sick," Maria said.

"Sick. I see."

"Yeah, it was pretty bad. I had typhus. Do you want to see my doctor's note?"

I almost didn't believe it. Wasn't typhus eradicated? All I could think about was I probably really don't need to spend a minute more with someone who has just recovered from typhus. My life is stressful enough. *Get away, Dr. Purdy.*

"No, that won't be necessary, Maria."

I thought that was the winner for "best reason for absence" until the following class. There was another student whose name was also on the roster but who had not yet appeared. I figured he had probably dropped out of the university. Lo and behold, just as class was about to begin, he arrived. I saw a new face at the door, and he walked right up to me. His voice became quieter with each word of his explanation: "Yeah, listen... um, I'm sorry I wasn't here, but..." he paused, leaned forward, dropped his voice, looked around then said, "I was with the police."

"You... were... with... the... police," I repeated his words quietly and slowly, mimicking his style. I wanted to confirm I heard him correctly. This was definitely better than even Typhoid Maria. All I could think was *If I have half a brain, I will quit right now while I am ahead. Forget a doctor's note, I have now graduated to rap sheets. Don't go there, Purdy. You* really *don't want to know anything further. Fabulous—the crème of the crap, that's my lot.* I am getting wiser in my middle age, and I decided to move right past this.

"Okay, well... glad you could join us." I smiled right at him and said to myself, *I love my job.*

"You'll have to get the notes from a classmate."

5 May 2008 London

> Someone asked me why women don't gamble as much
> as men do and I gave the commonsensical reply that
> we don't have as much money. That was a true and
> incomplete answer. In fact, woman's total instinct for
> gambling is satisfied by marriage.
>
> —Gloria Steinem

The trickiest issue since serving my petition has been finances. Victor is always reluctant to put money into the joint account. After several weeks of living with the stress, I finally placed a call to my lawyers to see if anything can be done. The situation is tense—tense enough, Anne called me back rather than the cheaper Sandra. Anne and I managed to speak after class yesterday when I could be heard bellowing into my mobile phone, "He is dripping money into the joint account. As if that were not enough, just as soon as he has put money into the account, Lillian cashes a check! He has the gall to pay Lillian out of that account. He knows me; he knows I can't stand having the bills be outstanding."

Lillian, another new name in my life, is Victor's solicitor. While on the phone to Anne, I was agonizingly aware that Anne's time is not cheap—but, then again, neither are the mortgage payments on our central London flat.

"Maybe I should start paying my legal fees from the joint account!" As I made my proclamations it occurred to me that perhaps my location—the favored café where my fellow faculty and students go—was not the best place for me to be having a conversation with my solicitor. I decided I best move to the café stairwell that leads to the basement loo. While walking to the stairs, I saw two former students in the back and waved at them with a forced smile. I had to pretend I was having a perfectly normal conversation.

Victor knows by putting only small amounts of money in the joint account, I will break and pay the bills from my own account. Actually, the fact that I have my own account is part of the issue here. My husband has repeatedly said to me, "You have money, Grace. You pay it."

By now the secret is out. He knows I cashed my second critical illness insurance policy and I am using the policy money to pay my lawyers.

Anne knows Lillian, and I asked Anne to tell Lillian her client is squeezing me financially and not carrying his weight. You know things are tough when you are hoping your soon-to-be ex-husband's lawyer will convince him to help you with the household bills.

My ranting stopped suddenly, however, once I heard Anne ask me a question.

"Grace, listen to me. Where is that money now?"

"What money?" I responded with a question to her question to bide time.

"The money from the second critical illness health insurance policy?"

I paused because, although I trust my lawyer, I was reluctant to tell anyone about that money. *That money* is my get out of jail card, and I refuse to remain in prison. The past couple of years I have become a reluctant expert on places of confinement—hospitals and bad marriages. As Groucho Marx said, "Marriage is a wonderful institution, but who wants to live in an institution?"

Marriage, like so many institutions, can look lovely on the outside but be a living hell on the inside. What looks like calm water can, in fact, be riddled with rocks. The most dangerous rock in a marriage is often the "resentment" one that hides underneath and emerges with the changing tide. If large enough, it leaps out to destroy the boat with the shifting tide. If smaller, you must wait until the tide changes again to escape. Sometimes I feel like I spend forever waiting for the tide to change—or for my solicitor to return my call.

My pause was not long as Anne waited for an answer. I thought, *Every minute I am on the phone with my solicitor, it costs me—a lot.*

As I answered, I said a little prayer that the money will continue to be there for me to get me through this process. Once I told Anne, she replied by promising to get a letter off to Lillian explaining the financial situation in our house. She reminded me that things are, indeed, moving forward and that we have our meeting with my barrister, Robin Sharp, shortly. After we hung up, I reminded myself that I want to finish reading the famous seminal English divorce cases *White* and *McFarlane* before we meet with Robin Sharp. I will be paying a lot for this meeting, and I want to be as prepared as possible. Not only will I read English divorce cases, I will have to brush up on my European treaties, such as Brussels II.

I haven't been working long with my lawyers, but I have graduated from the Brussels II class. In the academic world, Brussels II could have been named "Introduction to English Family Law." This is where I learned how critical it is to serve your petition as quickly as possible in the country you want to oversee your divorce. Now I am enrolled in far more advanced courses where the tuition is very expensive, as it comes in the form of legal fees. This upper-level class is entitled "Barristers: Juniors versus QCs—Which Can You Afford?"

The financial pressure increases daily, but I am hell-bent on getting my degree as soon as possible. I want that piece of paper that says I graduated, I am divorced—what the English call the divorce *decree absolute*—that is the degree I yearn for.

CHAPTER 7

Capital Contributions and the Dairy Queen

15 May 2008 London

And being in an agony he prayed more earnestly; and his sweat was as it were great drops of blood falling down to the ground.

—Luke 22:44 KJV

Today I met with Robin Sharp, the barrister briefed on my behalf by Sandra, my solicitor. All I was focused on before the meeting was what the meeting would reveal about what to do with the capital.

I arrived at Anne's office, where Anne, Sandra, and Harry were waiting for me. Anne asked me if Harry, a trainee at the firm, could join us in the meeting with Robin to observe and take notes. She assured me his presence wasn't billable. I told her I was happy to help someone learn, provided I was not paying. If not, then I should definitely get out of academics. So we all went together to the barrister's chambers.

When we arrived at the barrister's chambers, Anne introduced Robin Sharp. She proved to be a tall woman, aged about fifty, well groomed and elegantly dressed in her simple black Chanel suit.

Robin showed us into a meeting room. Seating was arranged around a large, antique mahogany conference table that looked as if it were at least one hundred years old. The room conveyed an atmosphere of deeply rooted tradition. Barristers have plied their trade in this part of London for around six hundred years. The understated opulence of our surroundings seemed an unlikely backdrop for an operating table to dissect my married life.

In front of four of the five chairs around the heavy mahogany table were piles of identical documents. As Harry, the trainee, took his seat, he placed his notepad in front of him. It became apparent he would be too busy taking notes to study the case documents. As the meeting assembled, I remembered today was going to be expensive. I plugged in quickly to focus.

Robin started the meeting by noting the "good news": by filing and successfully serving the divorce petition in England, we had established the action will be decided by English Family Courts.

There was also the question of the arrangements for the boys— something Victor and I could easily negotiate. No one can accuse my husband or me of using the children as ammunition in the legal struggle between us. My action was against Victor's failure as a husband, not as a father. I suggested to Robin that the most important agenda items were the financial ones.

"You mean the capital contributions?" Robin asked.

"Exactly, I mean my critical illness insurance money and the flat. I actually used all the money from cashing in the first policy to pay off the flat."

I refrained from saying how dumb I was to do that. Robin was being wonderfully legal and formal by writing "capital contributions." The flat is the capital contribution I so generously made. All I thought when I saw this on the agenda was *the flat you were dumb enough to pay off the original mortgage on.*

"Then let's move to those," she said. On the top of each pile was the meeting agenda, where both the flat and the money I received from my insurance policies were labeled "capital contributions." These were the main issues of the meeting. With that, Robin asked everyone to open to the second page of the agenda she had prepared.

"I must remind you, Grace, that there isn't yet any case law regarding critical illness insurance money in a divorce matter. Should this case go to trial, it would be a case of first impression. I realize we do not want to litigate this, but if it got that far it could make for a very interesting landmark trial. The issue the court would have to decide is how would it view this money."

The question has not arisen before because critical illness insurance is a new type of insurance product. I could not help noting Robin's use of the word "interesting"—an ironic echo from my earlier meeting with Anne and Sandra. I understand that bringing a case with facts that the law has not previously considered has a special appeal to lawyers. A trial would establish the legal framework within which the court would decide the status of critical illness insurance money in the separation of marital assets and if it would be divided at all among the spouses.

I pressed Robin on one of the precedents she had tracked down. "I see on the agenda you name a case here, *Wakefield*, with the decision by a Judge Wilson. Your note says it is a personal injury case. Are you saying personal injury lawsuits are as close as we can come to seeing how the court would view the money?"

"Yes, I am. One of the spouses received an award for a work-related injury. The money you received from the policies—totaling over seven hundred thousand pounds—could be considered as a windfall arising from the detriment you suffered, so we looked into personal injury cases. In *Wakefield* there was a parent who suffered work-related injuries and received an award."

I looked at Robin. "What did the court do with the money?"

"It was split seventy–thirty, with seventy percent going to the injured spouse."

There was a pause while I took in that information.

"I don't believe this—it's not fair! I know life is not fair, but I've given way too much financially and emotionally for me to surrender so much of the compensation arising from my illness. Are you telling me the only way I could try to keep the flat I have already paid for is by going to trial?"

"Exactly. It would be a first and groundbreaking. As you know, there are no guarantees. I am afraid your financial prudence may not automatically translate into hard cash. I realize this is not easy to hear."

The room fell quiet for a moment. It was as if everyone was giving me a moment of silence to absorb this difficult information.

There is a part of me that is so tempted to take this matter to trial in the name of justice, but I hesitate. Can I afford what it would cost me—financially or emotionally? What damage would the stress of a trial do? While I want justice, I know my bank account can't afford it. I was only a half an hour into the meeting and was wondering already how much money I had spent.

I did not want to go to trial without Robin or have to start again with a cheaper barrister. She is well prepared, very straightforward, and too expensive for me. Anyway, "cheaper barrister" is an oxymoron; there are reasons so few of the lawyers in this country are barristers—they are usually the good ones, and good lawyers don't come cheap.

Barristers like Robin are costly because they are in demand. They know how to best attempt to get the optimum results their clients want. A cheaper barrister could cost more by providing poorer representation.

I have already lost a breast and a flat to this marriage. How much more can I take?

"Right," I replied, "of course, no guarantees. What works in our favor?"

"I see this as a needs-based case, where we can successfully argue you are due more than half. There is your financial astuteness, the fact that, despite your illness, you have returned to work. This demonstrates you are far from "soft pedaling" through this proceeding and are producing all you can. The money from the policies is a windfall to you for your suffering. But I must again remind you—there are no guarantees."

Robin posed a question, "Grace, what do you want from the divorce? I think it is best to work from what you hope for and see what we can advise."

"I'm hoping to keep the apartment while he keeps his business. I sold my shares in Victor's business to his business partner when I was being treated in New York. I don't think it's fair if he keeps the business while the flat gets sold."

Robin responded to my disappointed look. "I can see why you want to keep the flat and not have to move. However, an issue we have here is that you have been living off capital and not income. From your financial disclosure forms, I can see you've been using the money from your current mortgage to meet living expenses. Your husband, from the forms we have so far, has not drawn any income from his business for the past year and a half. It's my understanding that when you were in New York, your friend lent you an apartment and paid nearly all the utility bills for that period. Realistically, I think you need to consider selling the flat and moving somewhere less expensive. I advise you to consider this as your best option long term."

Robin was fully briefed. She even knew the amount of money that would have to be paid in penalties under the mortgage penalty payback clause. I had not gotten that far.

All I knew was I didn't like the idea of selling and getting knocked off the property ladder. This prospect was particularly galling for me. I could have banked the original insurance money; at least then I wouldn't have needed to think about the cost of my legal fees. There was still the second policy, without which I couldn't have afforded this meeting. I asked myself, *How does anyone, especially a woman who has stayed home with her children, afford a divorce?* I didn't like what Robin was telling me, but even though I resist my barrister's advice, like many clients, I realize that I'm probably bound to follow it. I remained calm, but a part of me wanted to scream, "At my expense—at my bloody expense!"

From my illness I've learned so much about invisible dangers. I saved money. I never went out. I stayed home with one and then two small children, night after night, reading *Goodnight Moon* for the 150th time. After my diagnosis, I realized saving money came at way too high a price. What I lost was priceless: myself and my health.

I decided I was paying way too much money per minute not to express myself. It's twisted that it takes this much for me to feel comfortable expressing my mounting frustrations, accumulated by neglect and misunderstanding. Then again, I have been married long enough to know lots of couples never allow free self-expression to disturb the surface normality. There are partners who haven't had an honest conversation with each other in years. It becomes such a habit, it goes unrecognized between spouses who have become emotionally muted.

Legal fees, however, are visible—very visible. They will free you to speak up like nothing else when you consider what you are paying your lawyers. Stronger than any amount of booze I have swallowed or drug I've tried, legal fees can help you find your voice and fast. (Time is money here.) You pay great money for that platform, so you use it. I spoke up.

"I've contributed all that capital. He doesn't like to take money away from his business. I mean, in cash terms, he has profited enormously from my illness. Frankly, I think another problem is I've never been able to feel securely provided for in our marriage. Though he does everything to protect his business, he never puts any money into the house. Even before the divorce, I had to tread gingerly when I asked him to meet basic household expenses. He knows my family of origin in the States is very dysfunctional and that I've never been able to feel safe and secure in my home. He knows that this has been a long-standing problem for me—since childhood. But he doesn't seem to care."

Anne looked at me from midway down the conference table and said,

"I think another approach would be to note that he has been husbanding resources in the business."

"Bingo, exactly! Victor knows how to marry money. He can husband resources, but he'll be damned if he can be a husband to a woman. He conserves all his energy and capital for the business."

Anne chose her words to great effect. Victor's loyalty to his business marriage is so strong he maintains it even at the expense of his wife and children.

He ignored me so completely he didn't need to bother with filing for divorce. I'm the party who kept on trying, to the point where it nearly killed me, and I will be the one who must beg the court to end this relationship. I know that two-thirds of all petitions for divorce in the United States and the United Kingdom are filed by women, so this does not make me unusual. I remember, years ago, a male friend of mine explained his own divorce as "waiting to be fired." Guys wait until they are fired from a marriage.

"Anne's right—he is husbanding resources and milking me for the difference. I don't want to sell the farm, so to speak, but I realize I do have to consider this may be the only way to stop him from turning me into a broke Dairy Queen."

I almost couldn't believe what was coming out of my mouth, but I am fed up with Victor milking me like I am some fat cow. I got back to business.

"I have two big concerns. In the short term, I can't take our living situation anymore. It is very tiring and tense. In the long term, I know we can't afford a clean break, as you have all advised. The challenge is he is self-employed, and I don't know how I will be able to track his future income. Look how vague he is about his business now. He will always protect that business."

Anne spoke directly to me. "Yes, well, we know the living situation is difficult. Still, you are getting some breaks, right? It is my understanding that you are staying at a friend's house on the weekends and he usually travels during the week."

Anne was correct. Phoebe is away most weekends and has been kind enough to offer me her place while she is out of town. I have managed to live at our flat during the week while Victor continues to pursue his business affairs, wherever they take him. Still, while there is a certain humor to the boys asking me if we are going to feed Phoebe's cats again this weekend, her beautiful house is not my home.

"It's annoying packing up my stuff for the weekend."

"How about your GP?" Anne asked. "Did you go to see your GP to see if he might get you the name of a therapist? I did suggest that awhile back."

Anne looked to Robin and continued, "We thought having a therapist to discuss the situation with might help."

"Funny, I forgot to tell you that. I did go to see my GP. When I told him the situation, he started smiling. I asked him what was so funny, and he told me I was the third person in his office that day complaining about living with a spouse they were divorcing! Apparently, it's going around."

They all smiled. Even Harry the trainee had to put down his pen for a second to giggle. Well, it is funny—and true. I can't help wondering if the nicer your neighborhood is, the more hell-bent you are on staying put and trying to force the other spouse to leave. Evidently, we aren't the only unhappy couple in Kensington.

Just then, Robin jumped in, "Also, Anne told me you will be leaving for New York—in fact, Long Island—in a few weeks, when your semester ends. A lovely place for anyone to be in the summer, I might add."

I know my lawyers were saying this to get me to be positive. Still, all I could think was I'd bet my last pound, dollar, or euro that I was the only person in the room who has had the joy of living with someone she is suing.

Suddenly, with that thought, I had a flashback to some old episodes of the American comedy show *Saturday Night Live* and its parody of the legal system. One of my favorite skits featured an urban, professional woman in her thirties walking alone down a New York City street with a bag of groceries. The woman is walking along when she looks right into the camera and says, "I'd like to sue someone, but don't you need a reason?"

Then the voice-over kicks in saying, "Litigation myth number one: your lawsuit needs merit."

I would amend this to the updated British English version with a voice-over saying, "Litigation reason number one: *'unreasonable behaviour'*— could it be ruining your life?"

Then, of course, there would have to be a small disclaimer stating you can sue only your spouse for "unreasonable behaviour" and not, unfortunately, your boss. After all, if "unreasonable behaviour" could be the grounds for any lawsuit, the already heavily damaged world economies could be crippled even more than they are by the banking crisis.

I stopped thinking about the *Saturday Night Live* episodes when Robin spoke again, "Grace, if you do keep the flat, we would have to think about the current mortgage payments and how they would be met."

"Yes, I realize they can't be met on my part-time lecturing income. I also realize I am paying the current mortgage on our expensive flat he half owns."

"That's why selling and taking the money you get from the sale to move somewhere less expensive is an option you must consider," Robin said. "I also urge you to accept that, because you can't afford a clean break, you may be tied to your husband's financial fortunes and misfortunes for years to come."

"What about for the immediate future? Victor has earning capacity, but he has chosen not to utilize it to build up resources in his business. When does this stop?"

"That is a concern of ours as well," Anne said. "We are concerned that he may try to bully you into an unfair settlement given the lack of resources. I have written to Lillian to ask that he start contributing to the house again."

They then advised me to pay only the absolutely necessary bills, such as the mortgage and utilities. They asked me to reflect on all we had discussed and get back to them shortly regarding the apartment.

I will get in touch with Sandra next week and tell her I am going to sell it. I can't keep living with Victor, and I can't live somewhere he half owns.

I left the meeting and headed to the underground. All I could think is how can I possibly be paying all these people for advice that sounds something just short of horrible and definitely exhausting and unjust?

I wish I didn't have to sell my home. I've been through enough. I would love a Valium-laced gazpacho for dinner tonight, like Pepa from *Women on the Verge of a Nervous Breakdown*. I realize, however, I must stay sober for what lies ahead.

CHAPTER 8

Hairdresser House Calls

16 June 2008 London

> There's a lot more to being a woman than being a mother, but there's a hell of a lot more to being a mother than most people suspect.
>
> —Rosanne Barr

I am counting the days before I leave for New York and escape London and our divided apartment. I look forward to not having to go away on the weekends, albeit just down the road to Phoebe's. The scenario reminds me a bit of that funny scene in the movie *The Nanny Diaries*, where the mother tells the nanny that she and her husband are getting a divorce so until that is resolved the nanny and the children will be required to stay on her (the mother's) side of the apartment. The film then shows a piece of thick tape that looks like a cross between masking tape and duct tape. The tape runs throughout the apartment, across flooring and up walls. I am doing my best to remain in my unmarked unofficial territories, but unlike the well-dressed, well-heeled mom in *The Nanny Diaries*, I must exceed my boundaries due to economic pressure. I cross into husband territory when picking up and tidying—something I do often, as the flat is now on show for estate agents whom I've had in this week for valuations of the flat.

I'm doing my best to see the humor in the drama. Just when I think there isn't any humor left, something happens that I know one day I will look back and find funny. The moments usually come when I am getting really down about everything.

Since Phoebe was staying in London last weekend, I could not use her place. Down is exactly where I was yesterday, Sunday morning, with both of us in the flat. It was about eight thirty in the morning when I heard the entry phone ring. As a force of habit, I threw a bathrobe over my pajama top and looked at the video entry phone screen, where I saw a man I did not recognize. I said aloud, "It must be a mistake."

Victor then came out of Thomas' room, where my husband now sleeps. "It's not a mistake—let him up."

I was confused. "What do you mean?"

"I mean, I am expecting someone." I could not imagine whom he was expecting at eight thirty on Sunday morning, so I stood by the flat door out of sheer curiosity. The doorbell rang, and Victor opened the door.

The man saw me there in my bathrobe and said, "Hi, I'm Jay."

Victor then said, "Hey, Jay. Where do you want me to sit?"

Jay, I realized, is my husband's hairdresser. My surprise left me speechless and nearly breathless. We are in the middle of a divorce, he has been dripping money into the joint account, and both his lawyer and mine have agreed that we are cash-strapped. Despite all this, he has a hairdresser make a bloody house call at half past eight on Sunday morning.

Who does Victor think he is? I wanted to march into the living room and ask, "By the way, how much is your hairdressing going to cost me?"

120

I was sorely tempted to ask my new Sunday morning companion, Jay, if he knows I am paying for his services. I took a few deep breaths and decided to return to my room to try to see if I could discover the bigger picture or lesson I could glean from this.

It was impressive. Regardless of his financial or time constraints, Victor always get his needs met and does what he alone wants to do. If he doesn't have the time to get a haircut, he will get the hairdresser to come to him—and his soon-to-be ex-wife can pay for it. In theory, I could attempt to be vindictive and hire a masseuse, if I had one, to come to the apartment next weekend. Of course, I can't know if he will have put any money in the joint account to pay for the mortgage this month, let alone a massage, so I'd probably be burning my own pocketbook.

From my relationship with Victor, I have concluded that he is very good at putting himself first and I, like many women, generally speaking am bad at it. It's not just me but nearly all of my female friends. I sat on the bed and thought, *What can I get out of this? How can I turn what I see to be yet another example of my husband's overwhelming selfishness into something of use to me?* I paused and threw on some clothes. Thomas followed me as I walked into the other room.

Thomas started talking to Victor, but Victor said, *"Attend Thomas, Papa a besoin de se faire couper les cheveux."*

"What is your name?" Jay asked Thomas.

Thomas replied, "Thomas." Then Thomas added, "Who are you?"

"I'm Jay."

"Papa, why don't you go to the place next to the dry cleaners? They cut hair there."

While Thomas did not seem especially impressed by Jay, Rex was fascinated. His head kept turning from Victor to Jay to me, depending on who was speaking.

It took all my energy not to blurt out, "Because your father's sense of entitlement is way too big for that, Thomas." Instead, I settled for making the most of Jay's appearance.

"Ah, Jay, when you're finished, do you have time to cut my son's hair before leaving?" I refrained from saying, "Because I am fucking paying you, pal. Bet your client hasn't told you that." Something, however, must have been conveyed by the look on my face judging from the look Jay gave me.

He looked at me skeptically. "Uh, sure."

I returned to my room and thought, *Well done, Grace. At least one of your boys who desperately needed a haircut is getting one.* Then I thought about it a minute longer. Really, I had not done anything for myself; I did something for Thomas. Two minutes after pledging that I would start to consider putting myself first, I have been a mother and thought about our child, not me. Ugh—is it impossible for me to do this?

Somehow, by negotiating my son's grooming, I tried to convince myself I'd gained a small victory. The truth is my hair is still a mess and one of my lesser concerns these days. My husband, however, who has never lost his hair because of chemotherapy or any other reason, was in the other room getting his styled.

He is still taking more than he is giving, and I am running out of time because I don't know how much longer I can take this.

At least Thomas looked even more adorable after his haircut.

CHAPTER 9

Divorce Cambodian Style

26 July 2008 Long Island, New York

> I am a great housekeeper. I get divorced, I keep the house.
>
> —Zsa Zsa Gabor

I have not written in weeks, because it has been wonderful getting away from the weather and madness back in London. The boys and I have been having a great time here in New York, enjoying the sunshine and going on outings most days of the week. Yesterday we had some rain, but we managed to make the day go by with a trip to the library, one movie on the TV, and some grocery shopping. We've also had lots of my old friends come and visit—some with their kids, and some on their own. My biggest struggle has been to convince my father that Rex is still not old enough, at age three, to really learn how to swim; "Next year, Grandpa," as Thomas keeps saying.

Right before we left for New York, I met with a few local estate agents. I decided to interview a few to see whom I will use to sell the flat. I finally accepted that the only way to ensure my home is a stress-free zone is to let it go.

The resentment was everywhere. Perhaps this was a good thing; I could now identify it, having stopped either denying it or eating it. By June, however, every piece of laundry, closet space, and even rubbish that did not belong to the children or me bothered me. Money was still only trickling into the joint account, while a steady stream of legal bills flowed into my life. I am cash low, equity solid but stuck (via my half of the flat). Not an ideal financial situation! The whole situation has been challenging, emotionally and financially. It was time for some sun and a change of scenery.

Victor is still protecting his business. He leaves me to worry about selling the flat. He knows I'll do the work—as always. We both know I don't have the money on my meager part-time income to move, so I can't keep waiting for him. I continue drawing on the remaining insurance money to pay my legal fees. It appears my choice was between renting elsewhere or paying for my divorce, so the answer was obvious: the divorce won. As my barrister, Robin, commented, I am living off capital—and I am grateful I have it.

Once I'd accepted the need to sell, it was easier for me to give the process my full attention. Agents came in and out, estimates were provided to me, photographs and measurements taken. I selected two agents and instructed them to put the flat on the market upon my return from New York in late August. I wanted them to know I am serious about selling; that is why I wanted all groundwork to be completed before I left. They told me the summer is usually slow anyway, so they don't see my short wait as problematic.

Earlier this week, my friend Liz called to see how summer in New York was treating us. We chatted. I told her I was concerned about selling the flat while working when I come back in late August. Liz pointed out the university only employs me on a part-time basis as an adjunct and pays so little. She reminded me that my real money is in the property business.

Then yesterday I checked my e-mail and found Liz had sent me a link. I clicked on the link, and a headline from the BBC surfaced: "Cambodian Couple Cut Home in Half."

Then we have an image: a photograph of a house sawn vertically in half, right down the middle. The first paragraph explains that a couple in Cambodia have cut their house in half "to avoid the country's complicated divorce process." Apparently, the husband split the adobe following an argument with his wife. I started laughing aloud. It is a funny sight and one I can understand so much better now than a few years ago. Wow, those Cambodians get right to it. No time for duct tape and shift work in their homes. As if that was not funny enough, the penultimate line of the article stated, "A local lawyer told the newspaper that dividing a property was legal if both parties had agreed to it—but that it did not mean the pair were legally divorced."

Hah, so even after this couple solves the problem of how to split the house, the local lawyers need to remind them that they are not out of the marriage yet. There's still room for legal fees in that half house to finalize the divorce. I sent Liz back an e-mail:

> I love it. This is much better than any of that "you get the weekends, I get the weekdays" nonsense. My only concern for splitting, via the Cambodian Saw-It-Apart Method, is the impact on my 5th and 7th floor neighbors. Do you think the borough has a sawing split regulation exemption for divorcing couples? They should be a bit understanding. The mayor is always saying he wants to create new housing. I mean, do you know how hard it is to find a decent flat in this town, let alone in K&C?
>
> xoxo,
> Grace

After I hit the send button, I fantasized about how the real estate market could change instantaneously if all the unhappy couples in the borough of Kensington & Chelsea—in fact, in all the great metropolis of the earth—cut their properties in half.

CHAPTER 10

White Slavery

7 August 2008 Long Island, New York

> The events in our lives happen in a sequence in time, but in their significance to ourselves they find their own order... the continuous thread of revelation.
>
> —Eudora Welty

I got an e-mail from Sandra the other day. It was one of the few communications I've had from my lawyers these past few weeks. Sandra, the junior and cheaper solicitor (whom I like), announced she is leaving the firm because she's moving out of London. I responded by wishing Sandra well and wrote that I hoped she is taking some time off between firms. Anne has hired a new junior associate, Nigel. I'm certain if Anne has hired him he is good, but a client is never thrilled to hear that an established relationship is ending. Anne has instructed Nigel to use the summer lull to get up to speed. I know people move on—isn't that what divorce is about?

The boys left me yesterday to go on holiday with Victor. I was thrilled, thinking I would have an entire week to myself before I return to London to tackle all that awaits me there. I am so focused on selling the flat that I am viewing the First Appointment (scheduled for late September) with rose-colored glasses. The First Appointment is the hearing when the judge decides what issues remain to be settled during the divorce.

Anne has told me there is a chance we could use this court-mandated hearing as an opportunity to try to settle the case. At least things are moving.

Yesterday, while relishing the first few hours of my week alone, I foolishly decided to check my e-mail. I saw a message with subject matter reading "*35*"—the flat number. I opened the e-mail:

> Hi, Grace,
>
> I don't know if you got my voice message, but I have a woman who is very interested in a flat in your building. She came to the office and asked if I might know of any becoming available. I told her about yours, and she is very anxious to see it before leaving on summer holiday. She is an all-cash buyer, so I'm wondering if there is any chance you could arrange access via the porter and let me show it? I'll tell you more when we speak, but she is very interested.
>
> Thanks,
> Zain

Zain is one of two agents I'd selected to sell the flat. Right then and there, two hours into my week alone, it appeared my holiday was already losing out to my new career in property. When I looked at the message, I realized he doesn't have my phone number here in New York. The voice mail message was on my UK cell phone, which I haven't checked in a couple of days. I briefly considered avoiding the e-mail request and pretending I'd never received this information—only because I wanted a holiday. I was happy someone seemed to be interested, but I wanted to know how serious this potential buyer might be. I didn't relish skipping beach time to entertaining some potential buyer's curiosity. I realized the only way I could get an idea of what was happening was to hear the agent's voice. I could have tried to ignore the request, but it would have nagged at me. I surrendered. Looking at the clock, I calculated it was already 3:00 p.m. in London. It appeared my vacation was already over. It had lasted only two hours.

18 September 2008 London

> People exaggerate, they love to romanticize, and I was quite prepared to discover that his story was not nearly so singular as I had been led to believe.
> —W. Somerset Maughman, "The Lotus Eater"

Back in London again. I'm not sure where to start. The first thing I want to write is *to hell with bankers*. Selling our gorgeous apartment has suddenly turned into a greater challenge than I could have ever anticipated. These merchant bankers have just destroyed Lehman Brothers. This unprecedented collapse has caused people to go into financial lockdown. My agents are telling me that we need to ride the wave—after all, this isn't the first time we've heard the world is going to end. No one is moving. They are holding on tight to their property in central London. I am probably the only business professor on the planet who is doing her best to ignore this situation and insist it is not going to impact me. I need to sell! I can't believe I have to wait for my money, while Dick Fuld, the CEO of Lehman Brothers, sits on the $400 million he cashed out over the past eight years. Fuld runs a 158-year-old bank into the ground, trades other people's money in crap mortgage-backed securities, cripples the financial markets, and I can't sell my home that cost me a body part. Thanks, Dick.

Perhaps I should have known something was coming. Last week, I got an interesting e-mail from my father. The e-mail was about Eliot Spitzer, the former attorney general and later governor of New York State, who resigned earlier this year after a prostitution scandal. The originator of the e-mail was a friend of my father's who worked at one of the oldest investment banks in the world. The e-mail was clearly going around the financial community in New York; it read:

Subj: FW: Buying v. Leasing
>
>
> When your clients ask: "Should I buy or should I lease?" quote this example.
>
>
> Buying…
>
> The math on the Paul McCartney/Heather Mills divorce is as follows:
>
> After 5 years of marriage, he paid her $49 million.
>
> Assuming he had sex every night during their 5 year relationship,
> it ended up costing him $26,849 per time.
>
> This is Heather!
>
> Leasing…
>
> On the other hand, New York Governor Elliot Spitzer's hooker,
> Kristen, an absolute stunner, charges $4,000 per night.
>
> This is Kristen!
>

> Had Paul McCartney "employed" Kristen for 5 years,
> he would have paid $7.3 million in total for sex every night for 5
> years: (a $41.7 million savings).
>
> Value-added benefits are:
> * a 22-year-old
> * no coaxing
> * never a headache
> * happily agrees to all requests
> * no complaining
> * no honey-do lists
> * has two legs
>
> Best of all, she leaves and comes back when asked.
>
> All at 1/7th the cost and no legal fees.
>
> Sometimes leasing just makes more sense!

God, it was beyond horrid. It had so many erroneous figures and lies. "Kristen" is the $4,000-a-night prostitute Spitzer, also known as "Client 9," paid to service his penis. The gist of it is that, economically, Spitzer's time as "Client 9" (the escort agency's code name for him) was better value for money per sexual act than Paul McCartney's marriage to Heather Mills. I should have known the universe was going to have to do something massive to correct the arrogance and megalomania that has contaminated bankers.

I replied to my father and his finance friend, correcting all the factual errors, most notably, the exaggerated numbers of the settlement Mills received and the incorrect length of the marriage. The last line, claiming Spitzer did not have legal fees, was the most outrageous lie. What a joke! I bet Spitzer spent more in legal fees than McCartney. After all, Spitzer was paying his legal team to keep his ass out of prison for committing the federal crime of transporting a prostitute across state lines (from New York to Washington). The law is named, appropriately enough, the "Mann Act." McCartney's lawyers were fighting over his parting with 6 percent of his net worth.

A couple of days later, I was on the phone with my father. He said he'd sent me the "joke" because he knew I used the case in class. We had discussed the legal aspects of the case previously, as only two lawyers can. Laymen seldom see the facts the same way as lawyers. He said, "Hi, honey. Hey, thanks for sending back that e-mail. I thought that singer didn't want to pay school fees, but I guess the judge made it clear in his order he had to pay them."

"Yeah, Dad, he pays the child's school fees. The school fees are separate from her settlement money. But did you see my response, where I wrote the e-mail exaggerated her settlement money? It said Mills got $49 million. Not true—she got £24.3 million, so that's about $36 million. Did you ever hear back from the chap after I sent the response to both of you?"

"No."

"Of course not," I said in response. I continued, "Isn't it a bit rich of a banker to make fun of anyone for prostituting herself? Do these guys in finance really think they can be passing judgment on people for selling or negotiating something to keep a roof over their heads? Hah, talk about the pot calling the kettle black! They take our hard-earned money to sell the crappiest deals and products in the history of humanity, for what? So they can keep their huge homes and holidays and get the taxpayers to bail them out when they blow it all! Maybe they need to look at the definition of a prostitute again? Talk about selling your services for an unworthy cause. At least with sex you know what you are buying."

"Grace, really."

"Really what, Dad? I'm fed up. It's tough out there for us working folks. Besides, it's true."

"Well, you know, they really should legalize it."

"What—banking? They already have, Dad." We both started laughing. He was calling from work, and the other line rang; he had to go.

Some have described Sir Paul McCartney as a victim. I can't believe that anyone can accept that. Mills was as unprincipled as Oliver Twist—she asked for more. Justice Bennett's decision stated that they used birth control until they were married and that Mills had a miscarriage before her daughter was born. McCartney wanted the marriage and their child.

The other day, I read in the newspaper that McCartney's barrister, Nicholas Mostyn QC, is getting divorced. An article in the *Daily Mail* said Mostyn had split from his wife of twenty-five years—the mother of his four children—and was dating a barrister who was a widow. The article also stated Mostyn's wife had resorted to turning the family home, which was located outside of London, into a bed and breakfast while she awaited a final settlement from her husband.

The newspaper reported Mostyn had stopped practicing law as a barrister to become a judge. He has become Lord Mostyn, with the prestige and lower pay that accompanies elevation to the bench. The newspaper also included a photograph that showed Mostyn leaving the Chelsea home of his barrister girlfriend.

The whole matter depressed me. When I looked a bit deeper, I realized Lady Mostyn could have reflected on her husband's comments during and after the landmark family law case *White v. White*. Mostyn represented one of the spouses in *White*, and it remains the seminal

English case that stated "there should be no bias in favor of the money earner and against the home-maker and child carer." The judge ruled against his client. Mostyn has been quoted as saying, "I was acting for the husband, a Somerset farmer... trying to hold the line, saying wives should just be confined to their needs and no more, but that was the case that changed everything."[1]

This case hits home, because I have no idea how I will survive financially after my divorce from Victor. I know I can't live on my part-time lecturing income. I keep hoping there will be some insurance money left by the time this is over to help me get back on my feet. I know I am recovering, and I must pace myself. Sometimes it feels like there are too many balls in the air. I don't know where I will live when this is over, but I doubt I will have the option of renting out rooms. Anyway, I bet the bed and breakfast gig probably doesn't pay much better than being an adjunct university professor.

---

[1]   *Mostyn Powers*, Lynn Barber, *The Guardian* (The Observer) Sunday, 15 July 2007.

CHAPTER 11

First Appointment

29 September 2008 London

> God enjoins you to treat women well, for they are your
> mothers, daughters, aunts.
>
> —Prophet Muhammad

Finally, tomorrow is the day of the "First Appointment." It's been challenging in the flat this weekend. Phoebe had so much to do she stayed in town. Consequently, I had to stay in the flat with Victor. We both had to guard our tongues for the boys' sakes. It wasn't easy.

Anne rang me today right after I finished class.

"Grace," she said, "I wanted to speak briefly about tomorrow. Can you talk now?"

"Yes, great timing. I'm alone in the lecture hall. It's not often I get a room to myself!"

"Yes, so true. Okay, so we will see you tomorrow morning at ten at our offices, and we will all walk over to the court from there."

"Okay, I received Nigel's e-mail confirming the time and checking that I have a babysitter to collect Rex from nursery. Anne, I want to ask you, do you know who the presiding judge will be?"

"Yes, Robin and I were discussing that a short while ago. It's Judge Crichton."

"What's she like? What's her reputation Anne?"

Anne paused for a moment, and I can't say the pause thrilled me. She then replied, "Well, let's say she would be fine if you were on income support or some other type of state benefit."

"Got it." I nodded my head.

"Grace, don't be too concerned with that, because Robin is representing you. What I do want you to be prepared for is we may not settle tomorrow. I know you would like it if we did, but I would not count on it."

At this point, I decided I had all the information I needed for tomorrow. Calls with Anne are not cheap, and I sensed she was using this brief call to try to prepare me emotionally more than anything else. I thanked her and said I would see her tomorrow morning.

What my solicitor was politely trying to tell me is our judge is not going to bend over backward in sympathy for what is called in central London a "Kensington mummy" who is rapidly sliding down the property ladder. Judge Crichton is sympathetic to women on state support, but I hope she knows that trying to sell the sole asset that keeps you a step away from public assistance is no picnic either (not to mention that pesky mastectomy, eight rounds of chemotherapy, and several sessions of radiation therapy). I know if it weren't for my critical illness insurance, I would have been that woman on state support.

A "Kensington mummy" is not like an American soccer mom or a Chinese American tiger mother. When one says "Kensington mummy," what comes to mind is a woman who lives in the posh London borough of Kensington and Chelsea, is married to a man in finance—usually a hedge fund manager or a derivatives trader, does not work outside the home, holidays with her husband and children at the Indian Ocean, has domestic help, and looks great thanks to her high-priced hairdressing, personal training, and, most importantly, her expensive wardrobe. She wears her designer handbags to pick up her kids from school. This "Kensington mummy" leads a life that, from the outside, many would envy. It appears traditional and conservative and built around that rock-solid foundation: the nuclear family.

I, however, have lived in Kensington long enough to know that a "Kensington mummy" is, in fact, a high-rolling, hard-core gambler—probably even more reckless than her derivatives trader husband, because she knows she has bet all her chips on her husband and their kids. Her life is built around them. It's a high-stakes gamble given the kids will grow up and dump her eventually, leaving only the husband in the wager. She then relies on the marriage, and with almost half of all marriages ending in divorce the odds are stacked against her bet in the long term. This is serious gambling.

Women are expected and encouraged to be devoted to their husbands. English lacks a word for excessive devotion to your husband. We have created some colloquialisms in the past decade for excessive devotion to our children—*uber mom, soccer mom, tiger mother, Kensington mummy*—but never our husbands. There is always room for more worship at his altar. Curiously, we do not expect the same from a man.

I do my best not to get nervous about how I will support myself when this is over. Like so many couples, we have only one asset: the marital home. No matter how you slice a pie, it's going to get smaller with each cut. You can only hope to take the thinnest slices possible, slices that will get you what you need without destroying what remains salvageable.

Like most mothers, I believe I know my boys better than anyone. I am determined to work outside the home and raise them. I'm not going to be pushed into a corner by their father, society, or anyone else, for that matter. After all, my crazy family, society, or well-meaning friends aren't going to spend the requisite time with my children to raise them. I am struggling to even get their father to do that.

Not everyone will approve of my parenting style or techniques, but I spend a lot of time with my children; I do the work, I invest the hours, and it's damn hard. My illness and the divorce have sharpened my vision of what I need. I need to work and to be a mother. I firmly believe I am meant to lecture. I will not let the fact that I am a mother prevent me from doing so, or I will become unhappy—never a good thing for mom.

At the same time, I have two young children, no family nearby, and their father travels all week long for work. Like every other human being, I only have twenty-four hours in a day. I need to sleep for eight of them, so I can't spend twelve of my waking ones at work. It seems to me to be such an easy empirical equation; the math is not difficult. Yet, it is an equation so many seemingly intelligent people refuse to understand. The sad part is support networks that once existed for mothers are no longer there. What makes matters worse is that there are so few truly professional, part-time or flexible-time positions in the workplace. The stress on mothers today to be all things is farcical at best and toxic at worst.

I never could have predicted any of this when I married Victor. I believed we were happy. Before we had the boys, I didn't mind his traveling so much. It gave me room to do the things I wanted. Even when we had Thomas, things were manageable. Victor was so excited about Thomas's arrival. He sent out photos an hour after Thomas arrived. Somehow, by the time Rex came, he wanted to know if he had time for a shower.

One day at a time, Dr. Purdy. There is no point in looking back now—the marriage is over. It's time to create the new family landscape. Here's hoping tomorrow gets us a step closer.

30 September 2008 London

> Sometimes… it's better for a man just to walk away.
> But if you can't walk away? I guess that's when it's tough.
>
> —Arthur Miller, *Death of a Salesman*

The anticipated "First Appointment" day has arrived. I have discovered a new type of family fun trip—down to the High Court, Family Division, on High Holborn in central London. My entire new "family" was there: my solicitor, his solicitor, my barrister, his barrister, and Nigel, the new associate Anne had hired to replace Sandra. I have spoken (on the phone) with Nigel several times prior to today, but it is nice to finally meet him. As we had arranged, I met Anne and Nigel at their offices nearby before we met Robin, my barrister, at the courthouse entrance. We all had to pass through the metal detector at the security point. We then went upstairs to an anteroom to wait until the case was called. As we sat down, Robin made some polite conversation. She asked, "How was your time in New York?"

"It was great. The boys and I had a fun time. It was also very good to get away from my living situation."

I reflected that there was only one sad spot during the several weeks we were in New York. I was putting Thomas to bed one night, and he looked up at me and said, "I wish Papa could be here."

"Honey, I know, but he has to work. And we are having so much fun," I replied.

What I didn't say to my son were my thoughts as I left the room, *I wish your father could have been available at all.* Regardless, it's too late now; there we were in High Holborn, waiting to see the judge.

Anne turned to me and explained the procedure, "We will be in the back, while the barristers are up front. Victor will be on the other side of the courtroom."

"Okay, thanks," I said. I realized she was telling me the layout to let me know the seating should not be too uncomfortable, as Victor would be on the other side of the room. I appreciated her taking the time to explain this (and while that may seem obvious, nothing in life is obvious to me anymore).

After entering the courtroom, I had to fight the feeling that everything in my life has really bottomed out. My health, finances, and marriage seem to have all really fallen apart. Saying to myself, *Okay, Grace, snap out of it* does not work. I shifted my thoughts to the boys. That helped, but it also made me sad. While drifting down Sadness Road, I then called to mind the one guaranteed trick that always gets me into present time: my legal fees. Remembering how much this is costing me does wonders to dry my tears and get me out of victim mode. I started observing my lawyers and, instantly, was back in the courtroom, dealing. *I thought, This day ain't cheap, and it's only ten thirty. I wonder what the meter will read by lunch?*

After watching Robin and Anne chat, I sensed there was something that was occupying them. The First Appointment is a routine matter where the judge decides the issues in the case and sets a date for the next step, which is called the Financial Dispute Resolution (FDR) Appointment. Since it is a routine matter procedurally, I hadn't asked many questions about it prior to arriving. I looked at Robin and Anne talking quietly and wondered what they were discussing, so I asked, "Is there a concern?"

"No, we were just discussing Judge Crichton," Anne said.

"Okay, you can go in now," I heard an usher say. The next thing I knew, we were entering a room from one side and my husband and his lawyers were entering from another.

We all stood as Judge Crichton, wearing the traditional black robe, entered the room. She started with routine matters, shifting through papers. I sat in the back with my solicitors, watching the scene unfold. The judge then started posing a few questions to Robin, my barrister, and my husband's barrister, Mr. Southall. Both barristers were behind their respective tables two-thirds of the way up the room from the back. They both stood almost the entire time in front of Judge Crichton, answering her questions. I couldn't quite discern exactly what was going on as I watched the barristers speak, but I did notice Robin mentioned my health. Robin emphasized that the case has somewhat unusual facts as she discussed "the petitioner's critical illness and the policy proceeds." I got the intuitive feeling Judge Crichton wanted to see this case settled.

I found myself resisting the urge to say, "Yeah, easy for you, sister. Have you had your mastectomy money go to pay off the mortgage of someone who's forsaken you?" More annoying than Judge Crichton's desire to get a file off her desk is my husband's barrister. He strikes me as taking an exceptionally adversarial approach to the proceedings. In his presentation, he showed the minimal requisite deference for the judge. His loud, deep voice contrasted sharply with Robin's and the judge's.

Judge Crichton was persuaded to see why this case has not settled. She set up a timetable for the two next steps: a Financial Dispute Resolution Hearing and a Final Hearing. The hearing lasted about twenty minutes. After the judge left the bench, our team was directed to what is called a "mediation room" within the courthouse. Now that the First Appointment had ended, we were going to attempt settlement negotiations. In the center of the mediation room was a wooden conference table that held six comfortably. In addition, there were a few spare chairs setting below three windows along the opposite wall from the door. My "family"—Robin, Anne, and Nigel—flew in.

We discussed our objective in the negotiation: keeping the flat or at least the vast majority of proceeds from its sale. We also discussed what matters were negotiable, such as any kind of future payment from Victor's business. Robin then stood up from the table and headed to the door. As she left the room, she said she was going to speak with Mr. Southall and see if they could negotiate a settlement. I tried to ignore the sinking feeling in me. I could not feel optimistic about a settlement based on the amount of talk between our two barristers in front of the judge. You could feel the civil hostility in the courtroom moments earlier.

Once the door shut behind Robin, I recalled something Liz had said when I expressed my frustration with Victor and my living situation to her: "You are in the waiting room, Grace." Again, there I was, on another overcast day, still waiting in a room to be divorced.

I stood up from the table and walked over to the window of the mediation room. I needed to see space, air, and the sky—even if it was gray. After a few seconds by the window, I turned around and said, "I don't like his barrister. Maybe it's just me, but I think he was exceptionally adversarial. He doesn't seem willing to be collaborative. He was practically cutting Robin off when she spoke, and he was so loud. Who is he, Anne?"

"Yes, well, Southall is, well... I am not sure how to best describe him. Let's see what happens when Robin returns."

I was intrigued by her response. My own highly regarded solicitor hesitated to give her client a response about an opposing barrister. Well, that is an answer in itself. I decided to ride the wave and wait. It wasn't long before Robin returned.

The look on her face was, as always, smooth and calm, but not promising. She looked right at Anne and me and said, "It's not good Grace. Southall is saying essentially sixty–forty. Sometimes it is fifty–fifty, but then he indicates your husband will go only as high as sixty–forty regarding the sale of the flat."

I was reeling from shock. I looked around the room. After what was probably a twenty second pause, I said, "Is he out of his *mind*? Okay, well I don't suppose Southall is offering me back my shares in his client's company?"

The shares I was referring to are the shares I had in Victor's company that I'd sold to his employee while I was sick. His employee wanted to become a shareholder, and we needed the money—desperately. The cost of cancer is unfathomable; it impacts the whole family, emotionally and financially. Childcare alone became a huge expense for us. We had to hire three nannies: one for the weekdays, one for the weekends, and one for a few hours during the week to give our main nanny a break. I did not have the physical stamina to care for a walking eighteen-month-old child for twelve hours a day. Of course, the other conflict was that I would spend hours at the hospital in treatment. It was after I started chemotherapy that my husband announced he was going to have to find the money to hire a third nanny because our weekday nanny was saying she needed more help during the week. Thomas was at school, but Rex had stopped napping as he approached his second birthday. She worked a very long day and needed some relief. (I have been told by reliable sources many children sleep a lot, but mine never did.) Nanny, who had kindly come from London to see us through this experience, explained she was unable to exercise, see a dentist, or do things that required weekday time. Rex was awake from seven every morning until eight every night!

When Victor told me we needed to hire a third nanny I did worry about the money, but my self-righteousness triumphed. For years, when I said I was exhausted he would say that I was a complainer. Now, with me sick, he had to resort to hiring three nannies! I learned that he believed if your wife says being home with a small child is draining she is a whiner, but if your wonderful nanny says it you sell shares in your business. That is exactly what we did—or rather exactly what he got me to do.

So I sold the shares. The stress of not having money was definitely not helping me. I was desperate. I also knew that my minority shareholding in his business would never really give me a voice. What I didn't realize was that I was selling a bargaining tool that could have been handy during this divorce.

Fortunately, the flat—as well as the mortgage—was in both our names, so I still had a negotiation tool. Little did I know he would make it so uncomfortable that I would be sure to sell that as well. Still, he couldn't sell it without me, and this time I was not such a desperate seller. I'd learned that lesson, thanks to his employee. His employee, incidentally, only expressed interest in shareholding once Victor's company had turned a profit.

I repeated my question, "I mean, am I going to get back shares in the company then if this is his offer?"

Robin looked at me, "That was not discussed."

"He really thinks I am going to give his client more? I sold my shares, so now I'm going to split the proceeds of the flat sale with him? It's bad enough that I paid off that mortgage, like an idiot, with my insurance money. Thanks to me, his client can walk out of this marriage debt free.

If I had banked all that money, I could demand whatever I wanted right now because *his* client would never have been able to afford *his* fees. His client would only be able to afford some legal aid lawyer." I took a breath and added, "Of course, that is if his client is telling the truth when he claims his money is tied up in his business."

I could hear the anger in my voice despite my conscious effort to not raise it. Robin responded, "Grace, Anne and I are not going to let you agree to any of this. I know you had hoped for a possible settlement today. Fortunately, we are still on the court calendar for next steps. We are scheduled for the Financial Dispute Resolution hearing in the New Year."

At that point, I simply blurted out while shaking my head, "I can't believe this. This is bullshit."

I regretted being vulgar as soon as I'd said it, but I could not control my mouth at this point. To calm down, I looked out the window again. Though still overcast, I noticed the rain had stopped. There is definitely a part of me that has become a Londoner.

Robin looked at me, "Grace, we advise you not to agree to this. Frankly, Anne and I think you are wasting your time and money at this point staying here. We don't see any resolution today."

I looked at both of them and asked, "Is it him or Southall?"

They both responded in silence accompanied by a facial expression that more or less read "hard to say." Of course, I remember enough about my brief time practicing law to know that if a client makes clear instructions, they must be followed. Mr. Southall's client—the *respondent*, as the court calls him, and the man who remains my husband—has clearly not instructed his barrister to attempt settlement. Because there is no desire on the respondent's part to settle, I realized I was leaving the courthouse with two things to show for today: the first thing is a big bill for legal fees, and the second is a date on the High Court calendar this winter.

"Okay," I sighed, "well, I guess it's bye for now." At this point, I was on the verge of tears. I refused to cry, however, because that takes too much energy. More significantly, it could also be viewed as some sign of defeat.

"Where are you going once you leave here?" Anne asked.

"To work... I have a class at half past one. I had asked the department secretary to play a documentary in the lecture hall, but it looks like I will make the class now."

"Are you sure?" Anne asked.

"Yes. You know, being with my students is probably the best place I could be right now.

"You're probably right."

"Anne, what am I going to do if this doesn't settle? I mean, I don't want to indulge in that thought, but I realize at this point I must start to consider it."

"Yes, we have been thinking about that. Most likely our costs would be prohibitive, and you'd have to switch firms. I have a couple of solicitors I can suggest—all family law specialty firms with lower billing rates. One of them is Nigel's old firm. They have trained him well. When I send you a letter summarizing today, I will include some of those suggestions in the letter."

While a cheaper firm sounds great on paper, I am not convinced it is necessarily the best thing to switch lawyers this far into the process. The fees are high, but I am happy with my representation. My new lawyers may not be as good and, inevitably, would need time to learn the case. I wonder how many billable hours it would cost me for them to get up to speed on my case.

As we walked out, I thanked everyone for today's work. Anne reminded me that it is not unusual that we haven't settled yet and to hang in there. As I headed to the university, I could not help wondering where I went wrong. How did I end up surviving cancer to find myself the mother of two in an English courthouse attempting to negotiate for my basic economic survival? I started to wonder something much greater: Is it, I wondered, possible for women to obtain justice? Will we ever be treated equally? What would the world look like if we demanded justice and equality from society in raising our children? What if women put their needs first? What if all mothers lived like celebrity mothers—those very special chosen women who are able to employ a domestic army of nannies, assistants, and drivers? Having children never limits their ability to go to work, spend months on a movie set, or date.

Maybe that is the answer. I think about women like Elizabeth Taylor; she had *four* young children but, remarkably, had time to land *five more* husbands. Forget her looks or acting, *that* is impressive. Most single mothers I know are lucky if they can find reliable childcare and time to go out on *a* date—let alone manage five subsequent marriages! Later in life Taylor went around creating awareness and raising money for AIDS research, befriending Michael Jackson, but all I ever wanted to hear her discuss was how she had four children and managed her love life. That is the real secret from her I would have loved to know.

I voluntarily gave up working when my boys were infants. I don't regret that for a moment. I was there when Thomas first started walking. I recall the day, at age one, when he first drank whole milk. I waited until a day our first part-time nanny was working. I stepped into the other room to hear her say loudly, "Grace, he's drinking it!" Thomas had refused formula, but whole milk he liked. I was there when both he and Rex said their first words. It was precious time, their infancies. I am so happy I got to spend it with them and not elsewhere.

I am paying the price for that special time—I am a mother with little income of her own—but I don't regret my decision. I only wish it wasn't so hard to balance my postmarital economics with single motherhood. After all, a woman has to eat.

With that thought in mind, I went to class. Better keep the one job I do have and do love.

CHAPTER 12

White Powder and Supermoms

2 October 2008 London

> And what, Socrates, is the food of the soul? Surely, I
> said, knowledge is the food of the soul.
>
> —Plato's Protagoras

The First Appointment took a lot out of me. While I didn't expect a full settlement, I did hope that we'd make more progress than we did. The fact that I had to walk out because our positions were so far apart is what really got to me. I am so grateful I had class right after it all fell apart.

Simply approaching the lecture hall calmed me. My role as a lecturer provides a platform for detachment. Ideally, students can look to their lecturer for trustworthy information and guidance. Part of the role is encouraging them to engage not only with material but also with each other. I know from talking with my students and colleagues that I am not the only person present for whom our class provides a temporary refuge. My students have faced challenges, such as illegal detention by immigration authorities and parents who have threatened to kill them because they were marrying someone of the "wrong" religion. Whatever our struggles—mine or theirs—I know on a good day we can, for a finite period of time, escape those challenges and find refuge here. If we are lucky, we may even find a bit more of our authentic self.

Today my business ethics students were presenting their group projects. Group one took up all of the class time.

"Okay, we are starting with group one. They are covering Nestlé," I announced.

There were five students in group one: three women and two men. Although I try to balance the ratio between male and female students, this doesn't always prove to be possible.

Their presentation started with the company's history. In 1867, Henri Nestlé pioneered the development of a substitute for breast milk. He intended his product to be used to provide a lifeline for babies whose mothers were unable to feed them or had died in childbirth.

Using PowerPoint, the group provided company data, such as revenues, products, and share price of one of the world's largest corporations. One of them commented on how the company has been transformed since Henri Nestlé's time. It has become the largest food-producing company in the world, as measured by revenues. Their product range today contains everything from condensed milk to chocolate, bottled water, coffee, and baby food.

While I appeared to be just ticking the boxes to see that they were presenting what was assigned, I was, in fact, wondering what would happen when we arrived at the company's ethical dilemmas. Every company I assign has a juicy one, or several, and I'm always curious to see how the students cover it.

"Okay, Nestlé's ethical dilemmas," says a student named Lauren, who is standing at the front of the room.

"There are a lot of them. We didn't expect to see so many. They range from how it obtains palm oil to 'greenwashing' claims about how most of its bottled water bottles avoid landfills and are recycled. We decided to focus on its longest running and, arguably, biggest ethical dilemma—the marketing of baby formula."

A new slide surfaced.

"In the late 1970s, Nestlé got into trouble for its aggressive marketing of baby formula to women in the developing world. It actually led to a boycott of their products. The company was marketing its formula to women who did not have access to clean water. Consequently, babies got very sick when they were fed poorly prepared formula. Some mothers said Nestlé used saleswomen dressed as nurses to promote its formula. The company exploited the mothers' vulnerability, suggesting to them that Nestlé's formula was better because it made it easier to see exactly how much the infant was drinking."

Another student, Eric, took up the presentation. A new slide popped up, showing a woman taking water from a random water hole with a small bucket.

"The lack of clean water to mix with the formula is not the only problem. Even poor women in the West have been known to dilute the formula to make it last longer. This results in babies becoming malnourished and even dying if the problem remains untreated. Also, the company has not really addressed the problem of communicating with women who speak only local languages and are unlikely to be literate."

Another one of the group one students added, "Okay, we have two quick videos we want to show you."

He clicked on the lecture hall computer, and the first video started. The clip was from a 1978 BBC documentary entitled *When Breasts Are Bad for Business*. In it we see the late American politician Senator

Edward Kennedy at a 1978 United States Senate Congressional Hearing questioning a Nestlé executive about the marketing of its baby formula:

> Senator Kennedy: "Would you agree with me that your product should not be used where there is, uh, impure water? Yes or no?"

> Nestlé agent: "Uh, we keep all the instructions—"

> Senator Kennedy: "Just, just answer. What, would you—?"

> Nestlé agent: "Of course not!"

> Senator Kennedy: "Well, as I understand, what you say is that where there is impure water it should not be used."

> Nestlé agent: "Yes."

> Senator Kennedy: "Where the people are so poor that they're not going to realistically be able to continue to purchase it, which is going to mean that they're going to dilute it to a point which is going to endanger the health, then it should not be used?"

> Nestlé agent: "Yes."

> Senator Kennedy: "Well now, then my final question is what do you do, or what do you feel is your corporate responsibility to find out the extent of the use of your product in those circumstances in the developing part of the world? Do you feel that you have any responsibility?"

> Nestlé agent: "We can't have that responsibility, sir."

Senator Kennedy: "You can't have that responsibility?"

Nestlé agent: "No."

The second video was more recent. It showed a poor Florida mother whose sick child was taken to a hospital. She had been trying to make her child's formula last longer by excessively diluting it. In the brief interview, the mother said she didn't know too much water was a bad thing. She now knows she can't dilute the formula.

The lights came back on. Chris, another student member of the Nestlé group, described the initiative taken in 1981 by WHO and UNICEF to create an International Code of Marketing of Breast-milk Substitutes. Its provisions include not putting pictures of infants on its milk substitutes packaging. He noted compliance with the code is voluntary and not mandated by law.

"Okay, any questions?" one of the group members asked the class. They had been instructed to conclude the presentation with a question and answer session.

A student raised her hand and said, "So you said there was a boycott back in the seventies. Do people still know about this or boycott their products today?"

"Well, sort of," Lauren answered. "We were able to find information about their marketing practices. We were all talking about this last night when practicing our presentation. The problem is even if we want to boycott their products, Nestlé has over six hundred products, so it would be really hard to avoid buying anything made by them."

Another student, named Victoria, spoke aloud without raising her hand, "Isn't it much better to breastfeed your baby, anyway?"

Chris from the group replied, "Yeah, you know, I didn't really know anything about this until we got the assignment, but we saw some of the research and it's pretty compelling. It says breastfed children are healthier and the mother's breast milk has lots of positive things for the baby's immune systems."

Then I jumped in, "You know, Victoria, there is a lot of academic research demonstrating how much better breastfeeding is for babies. Breastfed babies have lower rates of obesity, higher functioning immune systems, and, of course, breast milk is a lot cheaper than formula. Has anyone in this room babysat and had to buy infant formula?"

A hand shot up, and I nodded to the student.

"Yeah, I have, Dr. Purdy, and it's super expensive. I couldn't believe how much it cost."

"Yeah, I don't know about here in England, but in Florida some drugstores even keep it locked up. I bought it a couple of times for my sister," said a student named Megan.

"There is another way women are disempowered through the use of formula." I had to tell them the whole story, so I asked, "When a mother breastfeeds, what else happens?"

A silence accompanied by blank looks took over the room.

"How many of you have a sibling who is only a year apart in age?"

Two hands went up. One of them was a student named Marina.

I looked up and said, "Marina, I know you weren't breastfed."

She looked at me with surprise, but from her face I could tell she knew this to be true.

"How do you know that?" she asked.

"Okay, does anyone know how I know that?" After a pause, a young man in the back, who has not spoken much during the semester, raised his hand halfway.

"Yeah, Robert."

"Isn't it because the hormones shut down or something like that?"

"Yes, thank you, Robert. Well done. Listen up, ladies, did you hear him? Breastfeeding causes the cessation of ovulation and menstruation."

The female students looked around at each other. They were clearly both astonished and perplexed.

"If a mother is breastfeeding exclusively, meaning the child has not started solid food yet, she can't get pregnant," I tell them. "So when anyone tells me they have a sibling only a year apart in age, I know that person wasn't breastfed, because it is nearly impossible for a woman to get pregnant so soon after birthing a child if she is breastfeeding."

I paused for a moment to let this truth sink in.

"It amazes me how many highly educated people do not know this basic fact about the female body or natural child spacing. We have become so comfortably numb to the sight of a woman manipulating her body to do something that it was not designed to do—something monumental, I might add. When siblings are a year apart, why don't we ask how a woman deceived her body to do this? We do not see the natural functioning of a woman's reproductive system as normal, let alone the sacred on earth that gives birth to human life. Of course, your skeptical teacher might comment on how doctors, religious leaders, and, especially, baby formula manufacturers never advertise this fact. Why do you think this is, Victoria?"

"I don't know about the others, but the formula makers want to sell their product."

"Should the formula manufacturers be ashamed that their marketing strategy increases the number of children born to women who are barely able to cope with their existing families?" I asked. A hand went up. "Yes, Erica?"

"Dr. Purdy, I know it's really bad for these poor women, but my mom said she could not breastfeed."

"Okay, this is a good point. I am not saying formula doesn't have a place in the world. What we have learned from this presentation is how a product that was designed as a back-up lifesaving measure more than a hundred years ago has now become the norm. We know that baby formula is a white powder made in a factory and that it is not a comparable substitute for breast milk. Erica, putting your mother's situation aside, less than half of all American and UK babies are being breastfed at six months. The World Health Organization advocates breastfeeding for up to two years. What do you think is one of the top reasons mothers cite for not continuing breastfeeding? Yes, Kay?"

"Probably because the mom has to go back to work. My sister breastfed my nephew for three months, but she had to stop when she had to go back to work."

"Good point," I said. "That's why many women don't breastfeed longer— it's too hard. We are exhausted by our stressful modern lifestyles."

Victoria interrupted, "I am getting my tubes tied."

Another student, named John, said, "Dude, kids are a nightmare. I love my brother's kids and everything, but, like, they are so much work. Honestly, they are not even really fun until they are like five. That's when my nephew became fun."

"What is the obvious advantage to bottle-feeding, aside from escaping the constraints of breastfeeding?" I asked.

The same student who said she bought formula, Megan, said, "The mother doesn't have to feed the child. Someone else can."

"Exactly, she can free herself from the constraints of nursing and get help. She can sleep. I think the sad thing is we think bottle-feeding is the answer instead of getting mothers more support."

Another student said, "Yeah, my cousin told me she was so tired between her kids and work, she didn't go out for like a year."

I then noticed a clearly confused looking pupil, so I called on him.

"Chris, you look perplexed."

"Well, I was just thinking, Dr. Purdy, about what you said about help and the mother. You would think that with more women working these days women would have more help at home, but it seems they have less than earlier generations. It's weird."

"Chris, I am really glad you said that. Have you seen the old American television program *The Cosby Show?*"

A student named Sam blurted out, "I loved that show."

"Really, did you like the mom, Clair Huxtable?" I asked.

Another student, named David, said, "Totally—she was the best mom ever!"

I paused. "Really? Well, I hate the witch. Why do you think I hate her, David?"

"I don't know."

"She has a million-dollar Brooklyn townhouse, a career as a partner in a law firm, a husband who is a doctor, and five kids. We never see a nanny, a housekeeper, a babysitter, or a grandparent helping. Hell, I'd take a carpet cleaner. The mom from *The Cosby Show* that everyone loved has to be one of the single most outrageous media depictions of a woman."

I paused for a moment to let my "slander" sink in.

"Maybe you communications majors can tell me what kind of manipulation was going on with that show? Somehow, Clair Huxtable managed to be a New York lawyer by day and a happy, loving mother, perfect wife, housekeeper, and cook by night. After a relaxing day practicing law, she comes home, cooks dinner for *seven* people daily, and then makes goo-goo eyes at her husband. Yes, I know it is just a TV show, but still—what might it reflect, even partially, these images of women? That is not for discussion today, but I share this so you can see how the baby formula manufacturers might have carved out a pretty sweet deal for themselves. The demands made on the time of women and men today are insane, and it leaves little room for parenthood."

Corporate ethical dilemmas were up for discussion, however, and not the exploitation of mothers. When asked if it has a corporate responsibility to find out the extent of the use of their product in situations that are life threatening to babies due to lack of clean water, what is Nestlé's response? Corporate ethics, indeed.

"I have one last question for the Nestlé group; based on your study of the company, would you buy shares in Nestlé?"

They looked at each other and smiled.

"Tell the truth," I said quietly.

"Well, Dr. Purdy, looking at its share price over time and the amount of products it sells—honestly, yeah, probably."

CHAPTER 13

Used Car Salesman and Uncle Jimmy

20 October 2008 London

> Everything predicted by the enemies of banks, in the beginning, is now coming to pass. We are to be ruined now by the deluge of bank paper. It is cruel that such revolutions in private fortunes should be at the mercy of avaricious adventurers, who, instead of employing their capital, if any they have, in manufactures, commerce, and other useful pursuits, make it an instrument to burden all the interchanges of property with their swindling profits, profits which are the price of no useful industry of theirs.
>
> —Thomas Jefferson, *Letters of Thomas Jefferson*

I awoke this morning at Phoebe's. Fortunately, she and her husband are staying in the countryside. Her husband, Alexander, is even commuting into work this week, so I have the full weekend away from the flat, which is now officially on the market. Probably because I escaped to New York for a month, I have regained some energy.

I'm managing, but the lack of a settlement continues to leave me unsettled. I am consumed by the divorce. Because of it, I need money now. As a part-time, adjunct professor, I am only paid for the number of contractual hours I work. I pray every night that one of the boys doesn't get sick, because then I would have to cancel my classes and, consequently, lose earnings. Exploitation of the faculty is a house specialty I am "benefitting" from, as I am now teaching three classes as an adjunct. However, between my teaching hours and the sale of the flat, I don't have the time to fight the university for a better contract. That battle will have to wait for another time.

Because we do not have a nanny at present, it was Victor's job to get Thomas to school and Rex to the nursery this morning. For the afternoon pickup, I managed to hire a former babysitter of Thomas's. She goes to college in the mornings, so she was pleased to find an afternoon job. She collects Rex from nursery the two afternoons he attends and then goes to the school bus to collect Thomas. She told me she'd be able to help until her course completes in December.

I know I need any support she can give me, taking at least some of the strain off single mothering. There are times when I can't seem to give anything the attention I would like to give it. I know I shouldn't ignore my needs while trying so hard to satisfy the needs of the boys, but it's hard. It's a challenge. Still, I can't neglect myself. I know what happened the last time I did that.

I returned to the flat late this morning, once Victor had set out on his weekly travels. After I'd showered and dressed, I realized I had about an hour before I needed to leave for work. I decided that gave me time to take some action on the flat. I rang Zain, but he was out of the office. He did take the woman he e-mailed me about while I was in Long Island to see the flat. I learned that she'd jumped at the chance to rent a ground floor flat in our building. It turns out her husband is handicapped and in a wheelchair. I readily understood. In fact, I was happy to see she was genuinely interested in the building. Since Zain was unavailable, I rang the other agent I'd been working with, Miles Traverse.

"Dr. Purdy, yes, how are you?"

"Fine, Miles. I was calling to see how you feel things are looking with the flat. There seems to have been a fair number of viewings."

"Well, we have had a lot of interest, especially in the last week or so, now that everyone is back from summer holidays. But, of course, this Lehman Brothers collapse is not good news. Everyone is a bit nervous."

"No, Lehman Brothers does not help. Perhaps I should give it more gravitas, but I have difficulty believing the world is really going to end just yet."

"Well, I know, but I'm afraid people are waiting to see how it will play out before going forward. Now there is talk about Merrill Lynch being involved. We are all learning to be patient in this office. Aside from the markets being jittery, we have the added problem of lack of supply. You would think the lack of supply would help but people seem to be in a sort of lockdown. It seems suddenly we have so little on the market. It's been very difficult for the agents. We have a real problem with supply. At least you have only one property to sell."

At this point, I realized this conversation was a time waster. The rest of his words begin to fade until I heard him say, "As soon as we have an offer, you'll know."

I hung up. I could feel the stress getting to me. You know you are alone when you turn to an estate agent for comfort! I called someone to hear, "It's tough all over, sister. Take a look around." Next thing you know, I'll be calling a used car salesman for comfort. Then again, if I don't sell this flat soon, living out of a used car is going to look awfully appealing.

At least if it was a car we were fighting over, I know there would not be room for two of us in it.

6 November 2008 London

> Still round the corner there may wait, a new road or a secret gate.
>
> —J. R. R. Tolkien

We continue to live out the scenario, the only new characters now being the walk-on extras coming in and out of the flat to view it. Still no offers. The game of *Who Will Put Money in the Joint Account?* rages on, even surpassing the ever so popular *Legal Fees*.

My lawyers and I received a letter from my husband's solicitor saying she is not sure why negotiations broke down so quickly at the First Appointment. Her client, she stated, would like to resolve this dispute. My response to Anne was it is not getting resolved if Victor thinks he's getting half the flat. We decided to wait a couple of weeks to see what happens with the flat before making a formal response.

I expressed my frustration to Liz the other day. She kindly said, "You are in the waiting room, Grace. We've talked about this. You will leave, I promise—it's just a matter of time."

I thanked her and then asked, "Why did the whole banking derivatives and subprime mortgage house of cards have to fall apart right after I filed for divorce?"

She reminded me, "It's not like you are selling here and then moving somewhere else more expensive—not that there are many cities more expensive than London. You sell low, and then you buy low."

"You're right, thanks. It's not like I am moving to Tokyo. It's just, all these people traipsing in and out of the flat, and still no offer—or no serious offers, I should say."

"You mean, you did get an offer?" Liz asked.

"Yeah—two—but from jokers who seemed to think I was in the discounted property business. Let's put it this way, when the agent called to tell me one of the offers, his exact words were, 'I am telling you this because I am legally obligated to do so.' Not exactly an ideal introduction to an offer."

"Well, you are not underselling either, we know that. Hang in there, Grace."

She's right—I am waiting. It will happen.

Patience is the world's most overrated virtue.

28 November 2008 London

> I am not young enough to know everything.
> —Oscar Wilde

I have lived through cancer. From this I have learned to endure far worse than lowball offers on my flat. Still, I want it behind me, and it is not. While there is tension and strain, there is also a lot of normalcy and humor. Because their father has always traveled all week long, the boys seem to be doing remarkably well. I feel lighter and happier during the weekdays when I'm alone with the boys. I don't think I fully comprehend all of what has hit me or will hit me. Despite this, I am clear that, regardless, these are necessary steps, so I soldier on.

I'm doing my best to find the funny and fun moments. The highlight of this entire month was Phoebe's annual Thanksgiving dinner party. Each year, she and Alexander have both American and English friends over for a fantastic Thanksgiving dinner at their place. When Phoebe and Alexander got married, they made a deal that he would take the day off and celebrate her favorite American holiday annually. Each Thanksgiving, the group gathers at their place around seven o'clock after work, and a good time is had by all. This year, while about ten of us were in the living room with drinks after dinner, I approached Phoebe to say I was going to leave soon.

"Don't leave just yet," she said quietly. I looked at her, a bit perplexed.

She dropped her voice even lower, "James told me he thinks you're cute. Don't leave."

Then I said loudly, "I'll help you get the ice from downstairs." We went downstairs together.

"I'm telling you, he thinks you're cute—don't leave. Don't you think he is cute?"

"Phoebe, he's adorable, but how old is he?"

"Young—why does that matter? He thinks you're cute."

"God, have we gotten to that age?"

"What do you mean 'that age'? Damn, I can't find the drinks tray." She was searching all around her kitchen cupboards.

"You know, that age where a woman has to start dating down. I thought I was still a bit young for that. I'm not even forty."

We both started laughing as she looked up from her cabinets.

"C'mon, he's a great guy. He's worked with Alexander for a couple of years now."

"He's great, but you know the babysitter needs to get home. I'm lucky I could finance one!"

"Woman, she can wait. I'll pay for the babysitter's extra hour. Now come upstairs and talk to James a bit more. You need to have some fun."

I followed Phoebe back upstairs with some ice and the finally located drinks tray. I chatted with James. We had met once or twice before over the years, when I was still married. It surprised me how much I enjoyed our talk. We exchanged numbers. We met for dinner a few days later, when the boys were with Victor for the weekend. A couple of days later, I was on the phone with Phoebe.

"So, I heard you went to dinner with James. How was it?"

"Lovely."

"Anything else?"

"No, lovely."

"Okay, Dr. Purdy, this is me you are talking to—what was the problem? You don't sound excited."

"Honestly, James is charming, funny, smart, and good looking. He told a great story about his family that had me genuinely cracking up. He is bright, he works at one of the biggest banks in town, went to some of the best schools and universities in the country, and he is surprisingly enthusiastic about his work—and that is where the trouble started."

"What do you mean?"

"He started talking about derivatives and how it's all about if you can figure out the spread better than the person who sold you the debt. I couldn't resist—I am a business professor—I had to ask. He was talking about the thrill of hedging the debts, netting. He got so into the whole nonsense. Watching him I got this creepy feeling, and, suddenly, it dawned on me. I realized this guy is so naïve, he still believes in the bullshit of banking—he's like a child. I couldn't take it. All I could think is he probably still believes in Santa Claus too, possibly the Easter Bunny. Then I was off in my head. I thought maybe he would have some good ideas on how much the Tooth Fairy should pay out these days. I am struggling with that. I meant to ask some of the moms at the bus stop the other morning but forgot. Once I got to the Tooth Fairy, I looked around the restaurant and thought, *The bartender probably thinks I am his nanny.*"

Phoebe was laughing and said, "Okay, he's young, but still he could be a fun guy just to hang with."

"Right. At one point, I was like, 'You know, James, I have kids.' He then said he loved kids. All I kept thinking is—*what?* Really, he spends the night, and I introduce the boys to mommy's "new friend" in the morning. I don't think so. You know, like I'll be nursing my morning coffee in a bathrobe and say something like, 'Say bye to Uncle Jimmy.' Anyway, the boys would probably mistake him for one of the older kids on the school bus. You know what I learned at dinner with James? Younger men do not work for me. I have been through hell, and they are still in nursery school—like a lot of men, as far as I'm concerned. They don't get it, and I don't have the time to teach them. I get paid to lecture on corporations."

As I listened to my words I recognized I may sound cynical, but it is my truth. There is no on button whatsoever for me with a younger man. It doesn't matter how good looking, smart, rich, or highly educated he is. Many men don't get how hard it is to be a single working mother; to find one who could understand it at age thirty would be highly improbable. Even if he did understand, why would he want to tailor his life to my constraints with the boys?

"But listen, my dear, you are a star for trying. I can honestly say you are the only friend who has tried to introduce me to someone. Most of the moms at the school have dropped me like a hot potato since they heard I'm getting divorced. But between the divorce and a possible move, I don't have time to waste on what doesn't work for me or who won't include me. Not that I have to explain that to you. It's not like your three children leave you any spare time."

Phoebe was a sport, as always, and commented she can barely remember life before kids—life when she actually read the newspaper on the weekends. She was kind and remarked that at least she'd tried. Then, most importantly, she reminded me not to forget I need to have fun sometimes.

I do my best to have fun whenever possible, even when it comes to economizing. As an early defense strategy to *Who Is Going to Pay the Bills This Month?*, I cut our satellite television subscription. Divorce rule number one: anything that is not necessary must be eliminated when divorcing.

This rule is, however, sometimes frustrating during those nights after the boys fall asleep and the only energy I can muster is to watch an hour of TV. Without cable or satellite, the TV is limited to only five channels. One night last week it got so bad, I caught myself watching a documentary entitled *Special Needs Pets* about a couple that adopt pet pigs. Just as I was lamenting the lack of stations, the phone rang.

"Hello, is Mr. Moreau there?"

"May I ask who's calling?"

"This is Sky Satellite Television."

"What is it you are calling in reference to?" I asked. (As if I didn't know—please, they wanted money.)

"We want to speak with him about renewing his subscription to Sky. Also, we'd like to tell him about our great new monthly plan."

"Well, no, Mr. Moreau is not home. In fact, he is getting a divorce, so he definitely can't afford Sky Television. He needs that money for his solicitor's fees... Good-bye."

I hung up the phone and laughed out loud. I did not doubt the company caller was probably telling her colleague, "You should hear what some crazy American lady just told me." Regardless, I enjoyed the laugh at the satellite television company's expense. I do, however, wonder if my response will surface in some market research survey Sky conducts later, when examining reasons why customers leave: "Customer explained money needed for divorce legal fees."

CHAPTER 14

Is That the Final Offer?

18 December 2008 London

> Nobody knows what is going to happen to him from
> one moment to the next, or how one will bear it.
>   —James Baldwin

Progress—finally. This week has been a whirlwind, and it's not even Friday. It started on Tuesday, when I was marking exams at a café. My phone rang; I looked at the phone and saw the call was from the estate agent. I hesitated to answer. I wanted to get the monotonous marking finished so my Christmas break could begin. I thought the agent probably wanted to arrange another after 7:00 p.m. viewing—"Do you mind?" I decided to answer. After all, as Liz said, my main business is property these days.

"Hello."

"Grace, it's Zain."

"Hi, Zain, what's up?"

"Well, I have some news. I have an offer."

I knew it must be decent if he was calling me himself rather than giving the job to an assistant. I put my marking pen down. I wanted to hear this. It was an offer—not great, but not bad either. Most interestingly, the offer was so specific a number that I felt this could possibly be my green light.

"Okay, that's interesting. Do you think they are serious, Zain?"

"Yes, I really do. I know the wife really likes the flat and, of course, the view. I also know they have two university-age children, so with your one other double bedroom and the spare single they think it is the perfect size. They will use one for a home office and the other as a spare for their kids when they are home visiting. I can see if I can get them up a bit."

"Okay, why don't you do that. Tell them my reaction. I will also have to mention this offer to my husband—unlike the other offers. I'll get back to you shortly."

I looked down at the pile of papers I was grading. Sod them. The numbers don't lie; my money is in property, not in my position as a part-time academic. For the first time things like finding a new flat, getting a new phone number, and calling movers flashed before my eyes. Then I caught myself. *Slow down, woman. You are not there yet.* I came to a crashing halt. I recalled there remains the outstanding issue that I still don't know what I might be able to keep from the sale.

Even so, if this sale is going to happen, I need to speak with Anne and Victor. He remains the legal co-owner of the flat, along with the bank.

I called Victor yesterday, Wednesday. I sent him a message first so he knew why I was calling him. We spoke, and he agreed with my assessment. In fact, when I told him his exact response was, "Hmm, interesting." Again, that word! In our brief conversation he volunteered his whereabouts, saying he was in Paris and would be back Friday morning. He also suggested we wait a bit. I told him I'd asked Zain to see if our potential purchasers would come up some.

Later this morning, as I was getting to the end of my marking pile, Zain rang again.

"Hi, Grace. Well, I spoke to the offerers and told them your response. They are willing to go up a bit. They've come up fifteen thousand pounds. I am not sure how much higher they will go."

"Okay," I paused. "I need to consider it. I realize Christmas is just a week away. I'll try to get back to you by tomorrow. If not, definitely Monday."

Zain told me the offerers had simply asked for a response before the holiday, when everyone would be off until New Year. I need to tell Victor and Anne this revised number tomorrow. Of course, any increase makes it more *interesting*, as the French would say. I am already feeling a sense of weight lifting off my shoulders with this offer. It certainly would make for an awfully nice Christmas present.

Speaking of Christmas, Victor and I agreed we would spend it together so the boys can enjoy Santa's visit. We both felt it would be unfair to allow the divorce to interfere with their Christmas joy.

After Christmas, I am going to a wedding. Yes, a New Year's Eve wedding—a real party! I told Victor how little Taylor—now grown-woman Taylor—whom I used to babysit while I was in university in Washington, DC, is getting married. Victor knows that Taylor's grandfather and my father were roommates at college a million years ago and are old family friends on my father's side. I was thrilled to be invited to her wedding in the States. It will be wonderful to see old friends. In fact, I don't think I could have created a better way to spend New Year's

Eve. Victor agreed happily when I said I was going to the wedding. He wants to take the boys to Paris to see his parents. Apparently, a few of the boys' cousins on Victor's side will also be around. It sounded like Victor will have plenty of support. Most importantly, I will be child-free for nearly a week!

CHAPTER 15

Happy New Year

1 January 2009 Washington, DC

> There is nothing like returning to a place that remains unchanged to find the ways in which you yourself have altered.
>
> —Nelson Mandela

HAPPY NEW YEAR! I am so happy to see the end of 2008. I am also happy to be here in Washington at the beautiful Willard InterContinental Hotel Washington, DC. While Washington is cold, spending this time at the wedding with old family friends was wonderfully warm, and the two nights in this fabulous hotel are a luxury I have not experienced in years. It feels like a bit of a homecoming, as I attended university in Washington.

The past two weeks have been a whirlwind, but I will start with last night—a complete blast. It was great to see my old gang, especially Karen, Taylor's mom, who has always been like a big sister to me. Neither of us could believe Taylor was *getting married* yesterday! I remember collecting her from school in Georgetown after class while Karen was at work. Why, I remember taking her to my dorm room while I was at university. How different that little girl was from the beautiful, grown woman in her white dress last night.

I am glad to be here on my own. It was the type of wedding you want to attend solo, because bringing a date would only be a drag. He would never know the old gang or half the jokes we shared. At dinner, I was seated right next to Stan, Karen's brother and Taylor's uncle. The first thing he said was, "Hi, sweetheart. You look great. So I hear it's over with Lance Romance, huh?" Yeah, you can say that again, Stan.

Today I am indulging in the peace of this room, with its sunny view of the Washington monument and the Capitol. Breakfast was brought up to me by room service. I could sleep in and use the hotel gym. I have no kids, babysitter, or husband to report to and explain where I am, what I am doing, how I can be reached, or how long I will be. It is bliss—who cares if it is cold outside?

It has been years since I have been to a hotel alone. I had forgotten how much fun they are. Since becoming a wife and mother, I have developed a much deeper appreciation for what it is like to have someone pick up after you and bring you meals you have not cooked. I try to refrain from thinking, *This is how my husband gets to live most days of the week.*

Christmas came and went in a bit of a fog. The offer definitely relieved some of the tension in the flat. It did get Victor and I to speak about something else besides the boys. This bit of dialoging proved helpful at the holiday. We both made a real effort for the boys' sake at Christmas. Thomas and Rex both seemed happy with what Santa brought them. Seeing them have so much fun made it easier for me. Why, I even felt a little sorry for Victor when he spent two hours setting up a train set for Thomas. Mind you, they and even little Rex really enjoyed racing the trains on it once set up.

We both explained to Thomas that I would be away for a few days, as I was going to a wedding in America. We said we didn't want to take everyone on the long plane ride, so he and Rex will go take the train with Papa to see their grandparents. He seemed okay with that. He even asked if his cousins would be there.

Victor and I decided to accept the offer. We both feel it is close enough. After agreeing, I realized I had to call our property solicitor, Guy Woodhall, whom I had not spoken to since we rented the flat out the year I was in New York. I wanted to make sure he was around after the holidays if all goes forward.

I also told Anne about our decision. She replied in an e-mail saying she told Lillian, and they both suggested meeting soon to see about possibly hammering out an agreement before our next court date in March. I also discovered from this exchange between our lawyers that Victor has started looking at flats to rent. We left it that we would all look at our schedules upon returning from the New Year holiday week.

So I'd better enjoy what's left of the New Year week. I'm going to spend the rest of today just walking around Washington before going to New York. I will spend a night there at my father's before flying back home to London. This whole trip has been such a splurge, but I decided it was best to spend some of my remaining insurance money on something besides legal fees! A girl should have some fun to show for a windfall.

I am glad I made it here. I needed this trip. Time to take a walk down Pennsylvania Avenue.

CHAPTER 16

Let's Make a Deal

13 January 2009 London

> I know God will not give me anything I can't handle. I
> just wish he did not trust me so much.
>
> —Mother Teresa

What a day. I started out early en route to class on this sunny January morning on the tube, riding the District line through west London. The latter part of my tube journey is over ground, which was pleasant today because it allowed me to see the sunlight—a precious prospect during an English winter. It also meant I could receive calls on my mobile phone, which is when the craziness began. The phone rang. I saw it was Zain, so I answered. Zain is my new best friend these days; I speak with him more often than Phoebe! After quick pleasantries about the holidays, he jumped right to the matter.

"Grace, the buyers are in a rental and want to move quickly. They're hoping to exchange in the next two weeks with completion a few days later. Could that work for you?"

My jaw nearly dropped to the floor of the train. After collecting my breath, I replied, "Zain, listen, I understand they want to move, but I work and I have the boys to manage. I am not even sure how soon I can get the movers to come. I haven't spoken to Guy, my property solicitor, about dates yet. I did touch base with him right before Christmas, but I need some time. You have to tell them it is just not reasonable. It's been my home for seven years. I will do my best, but I don't see where I can find the time to move in the next fourteen days or so."

"It's just that they are eager and want to get in, because I believe they plan on doing some work on the place once they complete the purchase on the flat."

"Zain, did you tell them I work? They know I have little kids. When I am in lectures, I can't do anything else. I can't interrupt class to take calls from the movers. Frankly, by the time my kids get to bed, I don't have any energy to do anything else. I know they don't care, but it is my reality."

As I pleaded with my estate agent for more time, the funniest part of this conversation was the speech balloon in my head. I refrained from telling him, *I also have that pesky divorce to manage on top of everything else.* I even refrained from allowing the dirty looks I was receiving from passengers on the train to bother me. The look that says, "Loud American. Can't she have that conversation somewhere else?" My fellow passengers probably do not see the charm in using a moving tube train as an office, but I do. I like it, because it lacks loud children or someone you're suing in the space. Why, I even like that I pay taxes for someone else to manage and clean it.

I know the buyers are a couple with two university-age children, so they won't get awakened at two o'clock tomorrow morning by someone demanding apple juice. They probably take it for granted that they can go an entire eight hours every night without someone requesting their time and attention. I, however, have just gotten to the point where I can take a shower uninterrupted, and that has felt like a huge personal accomplishment.

I reminded myself of the money involved. At least this couple is due to pay me good money for their demands. Curiously, they probably have no idea how much I want to move as well. I am not trying to stall; I need time. The buyers have the rest of their lives to have the flat—not to mention, they are getting a good deal, thanks to the bozos in banking.

I realized the real issue this conversation with my estate agent was creating was that I am learning to prove to myself I am not a superwoman. If it's going to exhaust me, I have the right to say no. The request is unreasonable to make of someone in my position, no matter how much money is involved.

"Okay, I'll tell them you need more time. Also, Grace, I called Guy myself as soon as I got in this morning and told his office all is a go. He knows where we stand on the sale. Grace, when I tell them you need more time, they are going to ask me when is the soonest you can be out. When should I tell them?"

I could not answer that question on the spot. There were too many imponderables to be resolved first. I needed to consult both Guy, who is dealing with the conveyancing, and Anne, who is handling the divorce. I feel that my purchasers are asking too much in their expectations of a date for purchase.

Nevertheless, I realized I had to say something to Zain, so I stalled. "Let me call Guy, see if I can talk to him directly, and try to get back to you on this later today, Zain."

I've discovered since this divorce process began that you don't have to be accused of a crime to need to desperately speak with your lawyer. Selling a home, getting a divorce, or negotiating a contract can all create the urgent need to speak with your lawyer. Indeed, I have learned that something as simple as buying groceries can create the need to speak with your lawyer. I now know very well the great divorce game show category of *Who Will Put Money in the Joint Account?*

"I have been buying all the groceries for the past month—when is he going to buy some? I think we should mention this grocery issue in our next letter to his solicitor."

I am almost to the point where if someone asks me the time, I want to reply, "The time… hmmm, you know it may not be in my best interest to tell you. Let me check with my solicitor, and I'll get back to you. Why don't you ask my ex the time? Why are you asking me? He has a watch."

After I hung up with Zain, I looked at the time on my phone and saw it was only half past nine. I surrendered. Apparently my life couldn't wait, so I accepted that the District line tube train is where I negotiate my deals. Perhaps this is something else superwomen don't need—an office or any space of our own to think.

I rang Guy. After I asked him about his Christmas and vice versa, he said, "Well, I finally did get that outstanding document from the buyer late last week, so things are moving forward. The question is where do you stand, my dear?"

"That's what I don't know, Guy. I mean, the agent just told me they want to complete within the next two weeks, and I don't see how I can meet that. Of course, I need to move too, but how can I find a place and organize movers in the next two weeks?"

"Yes, well, this is often the case. Now the seller wants to move, but it took them time to get some of the documents to us. You need more time."

As soon as I spoke, I realized how ironic this situation has become. All I have been doing is begging my other solicitor, Anne, to get me out of this marriage for nearly a year. All I have wanted for months is to wake up and have it all be over—the sale, the move, the divorce, all of it. How funny that now I am telling my property solicitor I need more time. I closed my eyes, took a deep breath, and then opened my eyes. I looked out the window and saw the train had stopped at Kew Gardens, the famous English botanical garden. It made no logical sense what was about to come out of my mouth, but I know it was what needed to be said so I said it.

"Okay, how about we negotiate exchange two weeks from next week with completion three weeks later instead of the usual month. Hopefully a quick completion should appease them. After all, until we exchange, none of this really matters anyway."

Guy asked me if my suggestion was realistic, and I emphasized it was time to move forward.

"Okay, I will move on that basis and will speak to you later this week," he said.

As we pulled into the next station, I knew the good news is this was really happening; the challenge is how I am going to pull this off. It was the last stop on the train, the end of the line. Only a handful of people were left in my "office" now. The entire train ride and morning commute had passed by me in what seemed like minutes. I got off the train, swiped my Oyster card, took another deep breath, and took a moment to appreciate how grateful I was to be going to the lecture hall. For the next couple of hours, I will get away from all of the chaos. My life has proven to me there are very few things we know for sure. I do, however, know the next five weeks of my life are going to be a lot faster and bumpier than riding the District line train through Kew Gardens.

CHAPTER 17

Barrister's Fees and Trial Prep

20 January 2009 London

> When people are ready to, they change. They never do it before then, and sometimes they die before they get around to it. You can't make them change if they don't want to, just like when they do want to, you can't stop them.
>
> —Andy Warhol

I am doing my best to stay calm and focused as the days progress. It would be nice to have a nanny, but the babysitter is helping. Let's face it—I can't afford a nanny now, anyway. My time is so tightly scheduled. Still, I am tired. That is the big challenge. I must maximize any moment I am not at work or with the boys to manage the rest of my life. Initially, I tried to tell myself I was like so many other working mothers, doing my best without a solid partnership or stable childcare to help, but I have accepted I am different.

I am different because, while I lack solid childcare or a happy husband, I do, however, have four lawyers. Yes, siree, four lawyers in the form of a family law/divorce solicitor, a junior family solicitor, a barrister, and a property solicitor. My legal bills are so impressive that I can't afford something as bourgeois as a babysitter. Why have help at home when you can have a legal team? Babysitters are so passé—anyone can get a babysitter. I am pioneering a cutting-edge new trend, redefining "the help" for the new millennium. Next time one of my Kensington mummy friends asks at the school bus stop in the morning if I have found a nanny yet, I'll tell her, "Not yet. I'm waiting until my barrister finishes the job. Do you have a barrister? I'll tell you, one day of her time makes the nanny's quarterly taxes look like a steal!"

My barrister was cause for another eye-opener this week. I checked my mail and found what I thought would be a bill from Anne. I was anticipating that she would bill me, since she'd had a conversation with Victor's solicitor, Lillian, on scheduling another meeting now that we have an offer on the flat.

Much to my surprise, I opened the envelope and found I was being charged £6,050. I didn't even have time to be shocked, because I saw right next to the bill the itemization reading, "Conference with Robin Sharp." All I could think was the conference with Robin Sharp, my barrister, was months ago. I paid this charge. Surely, this must be a mistake. I was too anxious to wait for an e-mail response, so I picked up the phone. I stopped myself from ringing Anne's direct line, because I realized I didn't want to get charged for this administrative question. *Best to go through the secretary. She doesn't bill me.*

I rang the general reception number at her office. "Yes, this is Grace Purdy, I am a client of Anne Clayton's. May I speak with her assistant, please."

"Please hold." A short pause, and then I heard, "Hello, this is Mary."

"Hi, Mary. Grace Purdy here. I'm calling in regard to Anne's latest bill. It lists a charge of over six thousand pounds for the conference with

Robin Sharp. I believe this is a mistake. I paid my barrister's fee in June, so I don't understand this charge."

"Oh, I see. Afraid I don't have the bill in front of me."

I asked her if she could access it. I waited a minute while she pulled it up on her screen. I could hear her typing on her computer.

"Yes, I see it now. Well, I would need to speak with Anne about this before I could say anything."

"I am not disputing the other charge for two hundred fifty pounds for Anne's discussion with Lillian. It's the rather more significant six thousand pound charge I'm questioning. Would you be so kind as to speak with Anne when you can and get back to me about it?"

A few hours later, Mary called me back.

"Dr. Purdy, it's Mary here, from Anne Clayton's office."

"Ah, yes. Hi, Mary."

"I have spoken with Anne, and it appears our billing department has made an error sending that bill twice. We are terribly sorry for the error."

Feeling much relieved, I thanked Mary for the prompt response. But after I hung up the phone, I found myself also feeling somewhat vexed. I can understand mistakes happen. What did annoy me, however, was this feeling that there seems to be no one in my life I do not have to manage—heavily. I even have to watch my advocates, who bill me hundreds of pounds per hour. It's tiring.

The very next day, I received an apology letter from Anne:

Dear Grace:

Please accept my apologies for the error on your last bill, dated 15 January 2009. It appears our billing department made an error that has since been corrected, and we are sorry for the mistake. (Please know you have not been billed for this letter.)

Warm Regards,
Anne Clayton

Fabulous—I am on a roll. A freebie apology letter from my solicitor.

For a moment, I wondered what it would be like to send out a bill for over £6,000 "by accident." What intrigued me most about the billing error is I bet there are clients of that firm who don't even look at their bills. Well, as they teach you in law school, *caveat emptor*—buyer beware!

I paid the £250. The next day, I received an e-mail stating Anne and Lillian have scheduled a roundtable negotiation meeting for the start of next month, before the completion date of the flat sale. The objective is to agree a final settlement, now that we know the sale price of the flat. The case remains on the court calendar for March in case we cannot reach a settlement.

Victor has, at last, told me himself that he is moving out of the flat. He has taken a lease on a new apartment starting next month. It is a furnished flat, so he will need to take only his personal belongings.

My situation is not so simple. I have also started to look, but I do not want to sign a lease on a flat until I know that Victor and I have, at the least, exchanged our 10 percent on the flat. Once we exchange, I will feel comfortable enough with the buyer's commitment. I can't make the commitment an earlier, because I am already committed—to my legal fees, that is. My insurance money is going out to pay all of my lawyers.

While I had initially resisted selling the apartment, I have decided it is the right thing to do and will benefit both the boys and me. I know that living the way I did for so many years did irreparable damage to my body. I need to leave the space that housed that environment behind me. The body's healing needs an environment free of the causes of the original damage. My illness has given me the courage to leave the familiar behind, because familiarity can be a dangerously deceptive toxin. It can kill.

I grew up with absent parents and so married an absent man. It was the familiar, and it worked until we had children. I have discovered the courage to look around and see what is happening. I can consider the emotional impact of a familiarity that is draining my life away.

The habits that support familiarity are habits that fix experience in a narrow mold. The person you become in such circumstances will be stunted, unable to grow.

This is the problem with complacency and familiarity—it may cause you to stop testing the water of your own essence. Chaos, however disruptive, compels you to test the waters of your own essence. It is like a megapowered tonic that immediately forces you to start listening to yourself.

My illness was the trigger. As I began to be aware of my personhood, I realized how much of my life needed to change. So little of the familiar I had lived with for years had been beneficial. My life looked pretty on the outside, but, except for my children, it was all artificial turf posing as solid, supportive earth.

As I've told my students, we all die someday, but I do not want to be on the early checkout list. I hope a new home will provide me the support and clean slate to make better decisions for myself.

7 February 2009 London

> If you give your trust to a person who does not deserve
> it, you actually give him the power to destroy you.
>
> —Khaled Saad

Yesterday was the scheduled exchange date. My morning was spent staring at a couple of clocks in the flat. I couldn't decide whether it was a good or bad thing that I don't lecture on Friday. By noon, I had yet to hear from my property solicitor, Guy, so I decided to ring his office.

"Hello, Dr. Purdy. Yes, Mr. Woodhall is here. Please hold." I took her instructions literally and did, indeed, hold my breath while I waited for him to pick up the line.

"Grace, congratulations, my dear—you have nowhere to live."

I burst out laughing, profoundly appreciating my solicitor's dry, classic English humor.

"Thanks, Guy. So all went well? I was starting to wonder."

"All went very well. Of course, I would have been happier if we did this with you telling me you had the check in hand for the security deposit on your new home, but that was your choice."

"Yes, I know that was your advice, but I couldn't wait any longer." I sighed, "Okay, great—onward and upward… I am going to be awfully busy the next couple of weeks."

"Yes, I imagine you will be. You know you need to be out by completion, or the financial penalties are severe. Let me have your new address as soon as you have it. Good luck."

As soon as I hung up the phone, I became aware of the nervous feeling inside my stomach. The feeling triggered a flashback to a conversation I had several years earlier, when working as a junior lawyer. I was on a call with the client while sitting in the same room as the partner who was responsible for the matter. The client, a Fortune 500 company, had decided they were going to try the case and not settle.

I vividly recall one of the client company's lawyers saying they felt our firm's legal fees were worth it and they wanted to try the case; he instructed us to prepare for trial. When I hung up, I looked the partner in the eye and said, "Okay... they want to go to court. I am going to go in the bathroom, probably throw up, and then start preparing this case for trial."

I think preparing for a trial is a bit like a life-threatening illness or a divorce—monumental experiences for which you are never fully prepared. Neither law school nor life can prepare you for memorizing dates, documents, and prepping witnesses. I discovered witnesses are the toughest part of preparing for a trial. No matter how many times you go over the facts with them or how meticulously you prepare, some will keep it together when being questioned and some will simply lose the plot. You will watch them give false testimony, forget facts, contradict themselves, and sometimes be downright hostile. We did, in fact, settle the case on the eve of trial for that client, but we went through many of the motions. Sometimes in life, you have to prepare for trials you may not want to endure. If you get lucky, you might find resolution earlier than expected.

I don't yet know how the divorce litigation will proceed, but I do know I must find a new home and quickly. I'm aware of feeling a huge sense of relief for the first time in years. We've exchanged on the flat. Things are moving along. Until now, I've been running from one spot to another, seeking some temporary refuge.

It's a much deeper sense of relief than escaping to Pablo's or Phoebe's house. Although money is coming in, events are moving at an accelerated pace. I can barely keep up. I tell myself I have done everything I can.

No matter how difficult the separation has been, it's still more manageable than a pathology report. Divorce is an awful lot like a pathology report—you dissect the marriage, figure out where the trouble lies, and discuss how to end it. Yet a marriage is easier to leave than your own body. It's hard to see why people resist leaving the misery of a bad marriage, though they do, often for years. Perhaps their marriages aren't that bad. Regardless, they probably don't feel as alienated or alone as I did.

As I said to Robin, I hate feeling like a cow that is constantly getting milked.

CHAPTER 18

Nowhere to Live and Russian Landlords

15 February 2009 London

> Old things are passed away; behold, all things are become new.
>
> —Corinthians 5:17 KJV

"Don't move to Fulham, Grace. We will find something nice for you here in the neighborhood." That was what Lucy, from Zain's office, said yesterday (Friday the 13th, I note).

Viewing flats seemed like a horror story at the movies. One flat Lucy showed me was nearby ours. Although the floor plan showed a good amount of square footage, seeing it reminded me how frustrating looking at property can be. The walls had brown marks around the windows. Lucy said the landlady is a busy barrister, but she promises to fix the obvious damp problem. My impression is that this busy barrister does not have enough time to manage her property!

The rental market moves quickly but, thanks to our friends in banking, more slowly than it used to move. While the world is predicting

Armageddon in the wake of the banking crisis, I remain steadfast in my refusal to plug into the doomsday predictions.

My divorce has given me a strange immunity to the world economic crisis. As I walk around the university or London hearing the dire predictions, I think to myself (1) my bank is still in business and (2) who cares about your bank when you don't know where you will be living next month? Of course, I must also acknowledge my bank does little more than serve as a storage facility for my legal fees funds. Perhaps this is why I can remain detached so successfully.

It is a strange time to be looking at property. The banking crisis was an earthquake. No one wants to admit we all knew we were sitting on a fault line. Even worse are the aftershocks like Merrill Lynch. The aftershocks have really damaged the property market. No one is moving unless they have to. Everyone sits and wonders—is it over yet?

At night, after the boys go to sleep, I spend the one hour I can keep awake looking at property websites. I checked my e-mail last night and found a note from Nigel:

> Dear Grace,
>
> We trust you are progressing well with your home search. Anne has asked me to remind you that in preparation for the meeting next week you must provide details of either flats or homes both for your immediate rental and an eventual purchase. We realize this may not be a final selection, but we need these numbers to negotiate at the upcoming meeting. Please provide them to us so we have them ahead of time.
>
> Regards,
> Nigel

I am nervous. Completion is looming, and I still don't have anywhere to move. To remedy this, I took a plunge and made two offers on two flats I had seen that were tolerable. I wasn't particularly keen on either place, but I kept hearing Guy's words in my head, *Congratulations, you have nowhere to live.* Both offers were a third below the monthly rental asking price. I decided to test the market. I realized if I am selling low, I have to rent low.

Both estate agents were skeptical of my low offer. They both said, "Oh, I don't know if the landlord will accept that, but I will put it forward."

Yesterday the agent on one rang me back. "Dr. Purdy, I have spoken with the landlord. He has accepted your offer."

"Okay, great—well, listen, I am busy right now. I will have to ring you back."

I figure I have nothing to lose; the odds are high that the landlord is bleeding on his or her mortgage. I'd let the agents know I am selling my home and need to move quickly, cash in hand. Still, I need more time, as I am still hoping to find something better.

This morning I collected some particulars on the flats I've seen and rang the moving company I used years ago. I decided I better get movers lined up, since they need more than five days of notice. When I called, I reminded them that they had moved me years ago. Their employee, Maria, found me in their system. She asked a question, "What day are you moving?"

The question actually threw me off guard. I am so consumed with rapidly approaching deadline for finding a flat that I have fallen under the impression that "very soon" is an acceptable answer. I realize "Oh, any day now—you know the divorce is really coming along" is probably not the answer the moving company has in mind.

"Ummm, well, actually, I am not certain of the exact date. Is that a problem?" I did assure her that I will definitely be moving but am waiting for my landlord to confirm. "I should know in the next day or so. I am, I um, I am being cautious, that's all. Hate to leave things to the last minute." I salvaged the call by saying, "Can I get right back to you on that?"

"We usually need a move date to move people," she calmly replied. She has obviously dealt with a lot of stressed-out people extensively in her career.

I looked at the calendar and picked a date. "Okay, how about the twenty-fourth of March?" It looked as good a date as any.

"Let me see. Please hold."

She returned to the line to say that date worked. She asked a few routine questions and said she would send someone in two days to do the estimate. She then added that at least ten days' notice is needed to get the parking suspension permits for her moving trucks from the borough.

"Okay, so for the mover's parking suspension, we need your new address. Can you give it to me, please?"

I was in trouble again. "My new address. You want to know my new address?"

I was sorely tempted at this point to confess the whole story to my new friend, Maria the moving agent. I realized I was really sounding like an idiot. Should I start with breast cancer or cut right to my soon-to-be ex has a fire under my ass and I've got to sell this place fast?

I need the money, sister. I am not sure where I'm going, but at least I am getting out. I wondered if the "I need to speak with my lawyer first" response could work. Hmm, it was tempting. Maybe if Maria spoke with my lawyers she would see how I've ended up making the dumbest phone call of the year to the company. I have called a moving company and do not know what day I am moving or where I am moving to. I have, however, lived in Europe long enough to know you better book movers at least two weeks in advance or you won't have any help on moving day. I needed to say something.

"Okay, well, um it's the landlord. I want to confirm with him again. You see, I looked at a couple of his properties, and part of what I'm waiting to hear is which one is available sooner. Do you want an address and if we need to change it I'll let you know?"

This fictitious landlord of mine was getting a bigger story by the second. My mind raced ahead, and I thought, *If I need to mention him again, I could make him a Russian.* I have lived in London long enough to have developed an appreciation for how celebrated the Russians are for anything vague and dodgy. If you want to cover up something, use a Russian. If you want to impress a Russian, tell them everything is VIP. "Oh, only the VIPs go there." Russians love to be told they are important and to believe they are superior to other human beings. Something happened to them living all those years in crap communist housing. They've been so twisted and abused, that tribe makes New Yorkers look lazy and anticompetitive.

Maria settles for a postcode and tells me to ring her back later in the week with an exact address.

"Okay, great," I say. Just as she was about to hang up, I asked, "One last question—do you keep items in storage immediately after the move, in case there is a slight delay between the moving out date and the moving in date?"

Maria confirmed that can be done at a price. "But, again, the company needs that information in advance, so please let it be known if that is the situation."

Of course, that won't be me, because I am just waiting to hear back from my Russian landlord any minute now, thank you very much. I hung up the phone and sighed.

I may not know where I am moving, but at least I finally know I *am* moving and the movers are in place—progress!

CHAPTER 19

Clients and Penne Pasta

18 February 2009 London

Uphold me according unto thy word, that I may live:
and let me not be ashamed of my hope.
—Psalm 119: 116 KJV

The good news first: Victor has moved out! I was starting to wonder if we would be one of those super loser couples who are legally divorced but still living in the same apartment. This thought had entered my optimistic mind earlier, when I received a letter confirming a roundtable meeting with Victor, myself, Victor's solicitor, Lillian, and Anne for next month. The letter instructed me to arrange childcare, as we will be attempting to negotiate a final settlement and the meeting could be long. We remain on the court calendar in case our efforts fail again.

Victor has taken a flat about two miles away in Paddington. All I know is Thomas and Rex went there on Saturday night and seemed to have a great time. Apparently it has a very large TV, something the boys seemed to find fabulous. Thomas has discovered video games and tells me the new big screen makes watching *Tom and Jerry* cartoons so much fun.

Well, now for the bad news: I knew I had to tell the boys we were moving. On Monday, after Thomas finished school and Rex was home from nursery, I announced we were going out to get pizza for dinner. I knew if I had to tell them when we were in the flat, too many memories would come flooding through me and I would probably start to cry. I wish the boys didn't have to move. Still, Thomas was especially pleased to hear pizza was on the menu for dinner.

As we sat down at the table, Thomas said to me, "Mom, why do girls always do that?"

"Do what, honey?"

"Smile and wave at me."

I turned my head and saw a young woman, probably in her late twenties, at another table waving to Thomas. I wasn't sure how to explain to him that women wave because they think he's adorable. You can't exactly say to a five-year-old "chicks dig cute kids." Then I thought, maybe you can.

"Honey, it's because she thinks you're cute and she probably doesn't have any kids at home. She is young, sweetie, that's all. She probably wants to be a mom someday. You don't have to talk to her."

At that point, the waiter came over and asked what we wanted. Because I was with the boys, especially because of Rex, I ordered drinks and food in one shot. An almost-three-year-old's patience to sit still in a chair is a very finite period of time.

Thomas ordered apple juice and pizza. I then asked Rex, "Rex, apple juice or water? Which do you want to drink, sweetie?"

"Apple juice."

"Okay, and what do you want to eat? Pizza or penne pasta?"

Rex loves penne pasta. He says it so sweetly around the flat often, "Penne pasta, penne pasta."

He paused and, after clearly contemplating this great existential question, said, "I want penne pasta."

Even after all these years of parenting, it still amazes me how much kids love the same thing repeatedly and hate change. I wanted to say, "Rex, that's the fifth time you've had penne pasta this week. Are you sure you don't want to jazz up your life and try a pizza?" Then I remembered, Rex is only three and his life is about to be "jazzed up" significantly these next few months. He would have had every right to look at me and say, "You really think you can justify taking away my comfort food? Perhaps you haven't noticed that my parents are caught up in their self-inflicted drama? Mom, give me my penne pasta and worry about your own damn dinner."

I knew I had to broach the tough subject after we ordered. I wanted to get it out of the way, so I could move on to eating once the food arrived.

"Okay, guys, well you know how we are selling the flat to that couple? Well, they are moving into it in a few more days, so we have to leave by then. The good news is I found a great new apartment super close by. You can even see our building from the new flat's kitchen window."

I gave my best "isn't that super cool," Oscar-winning performance. Before the news could really digest, my phone rang. It was Anne's office, I could tell from the number, so I thought I'd better answer this.

"Hello?"

"Dr. Purdy?"

It was Nigel, from Anne Clayton's office. I had a less-than-one-minute conversation with Nigel reminding me about the upcoming meeting and ensuring I have childcare in place. I thanked him and returned to my meal with the boys.

"Who was that, Mom?" Thomas asked.

"That was Nigel."

"Who's Nigel?"

"A friend."

"Do I know Nigel?"

I didn't want to lie and have to create a fictitious friend, so I thought I better set the matter straight with Thomas.

"No, he is not really a friend. He is someone who is doing some work for me. I'm his client, Thomas."

I thought I could pull a fast one and throw around some fancy words and be done with the questions. My son, however, saw through this. He then asked, "What's a client?"

I started to become even more nervous. Dinner was getting tougher by the moment.

Suddenly Rex said, "Client, what's a client?"

Why, oh why, did Rex decide to make this the newest word in his growing vocabulary? God, please, the last thing I need is for Rex to be at Victor's place next weekend chanting "client." Before you know it, I will be explaining mediation to Thomas.

"A client is someone who pays someone to do something for them. Like when we go to the dry cleaners to get Papa's shirts. We are the client—we pay the dry cleaners to clean the shirts."

"Oh," Thomas said and then, "I like our flat. Do we have to move?"

I fudged it a bit here, not knowing how to reply. "Well, Thomas, we have lived there for years. If we were to stay, Mom would have to repaint the rooms, get new carpets—we haven't done any work on the place since you were a baby. Also, the tenants did some minor damage when we were in New York, so we decided it's better to sell and find a brand new place. Okay?"

Just then his pizza arrived, and he started eating. He surprised me by changing the topic and talking about school. I wasn't sure what he was really thinking, but I was too scared to go there. I was thrilled to talk about his friend, Pierre, and how the teacher was upset with Pierre at school earlier.

Only time will tell with the boys. I wish we didn't have to leave either, but I have no choice. We can't afford the flat; perhaps we never could. *No choice means no room for guilt, Dr. Purdy. Move on.*

CHAPTER 20

Balance to the Phoenix

12 March 2009 London

> You's got to pull yourself together and think how you
> can win. You always been the winner. Ain't no time to
> be a woman now.
>
> —James Baldwin, *The Amen Corner*

In the course of my experience with marriage and motherhood, I have discovered that love has nothing to do with what a man promises you. What he gives materially is much less important than what he is able to give emotionally. A partner demonstrates his or her love by showing you what he or she is prepared to give up for you. I moved across an ocean and came up empty-handed on all counts.

This is what I learned from yesterday's roundtable negotiations. As I sat there for hours, I could almost hear the song "Heart Like a Wheel" playing:

> *But I can't understand*
> *Oh please, God, hold my hand*
> *Why it had to happen to me?*

"Why do you think he wants this money?" Nigel posed the question. I shared the confusion it implied. Victor kept insisting he needed a six-figure cut from the sale of the flat. I turned around from the conference room window and looked at Nigel, who continued, "He seems to be so set on getting it. Why? I can understand he wants his business, but the flat? Why this money from the flat sale?" Nigel looked genuinely perplexed. His expression was one of bewilderment.

I answered him from the window, "I don't know. I've given up trying to figure him out. All I know is I don't have a big income, and I need that money."

By now it was six thirty in the evening, and we had already been at this for a few of hours. Like tennis players, we went back and forth volleying. There is downtime while one side reviews the offer presented by the other party and then hits it back.

We were all at Anne's office in High Holborn, just down the road from the Royal Courts of Justice. The cold, gray winter's day had now turned dark. I stared out the window of my solicitor's conference room, where I had been sitting with Nigel for hours. Since he joined the team, he has done a good job of learning the details of the case. Now the negotiations had hit sticky ground; we had become mired in the question of dividing the money from the sale of the apartment. Anne had been away discussing the issue with Victor's solicitor. Nigel and I had nothing to do but wait.

As Nigel and I waited, I looked out over London and did what I swore I would not do—I looked back. I thought of our wedding day and what I would now tell my younger self. I thought that, for all my veneer of city sophistication, I had been a naïve child. I never would have imagined that day would lead me to a conference room in central London negotiating, indeed, imploring him to let me leave this marriage.

The demands he was making were unfair. He was refusing to see that my financial difficulties were at least as important as his. I thought about all I'd contributed to our marriage. We'd bought the flat we were now fighting over as a wreck. I'd found a builder to renovate it. I'd worked on the flat while still nursing Thomas. Consequently, I didn't sleep through the night for over a year.

Sadly, I know so few people on earth really understand that. Most women in the West are too exhausted to continue breastfeeding past a few weeks—three months maximum. People will tell you they've had sleepless nights and think it is the same. It isn't. It's more like not sleeping and then working out at 2:00 a.m. every night for a year, because nursing burns so many calories. It seems to me a bitter irony that the flat I worked on while "not working" has turned into the big battle in this divorce.

I'd even been dumb enough to sign the papers taking a second (though smaller) mortgage on the property. How could I have agreed to that? I concluded I was not of sound mind and body, having just finished eight rounds of chemotherapy and twenty-five rounds of radiation. In addition, I was living almost alone with a five-year-old and a two-year-old. Considering the nasty set of circumstances, it was amazing I functioned at all.

Fortunately, perhaps, my walk down Brutal Memories Lane was interrupted by a knock on the conference room door. When it opened, Harry entered. Harry, the junior trainee solicitor who was with us the day we first met Robin Sharp, was carrying a few documents.

"Anne asked me to bring in these copies," he said as he looked at Nigel. Then his eyes cast over to me. "Hi, Dr. Purdy. How are you?"

"Honestly, exasperated and still fighting about the flat." I paused and then asked, "Does every client feel this way when they get divorced—the utter disbelief?"

"Really, Dr. Purdy, don't take this the wrong way, but I've seen so much worse. I mean, I once saw a couple fight over who gets the George Michael DVD."

I had to repeat what I heard. "They paid legal fees to fight over who got the George Michael DVD?"

"Correct."

I laughed, "Well, I hope it was the deluxe box set!"

With that, Harry left the conference room, and I suddenly felt an increase in my dignity.

A few minutes later, the conference door opened again. This time, Anne entered. She shut the door, looked at me with a grave face, and said, "He's insisting on the money."

Nigel jumped in, "Why?"

I was comforted he'd asked and not me. I took some solace that even my lawyer found this perplexing.

Anne replied, "He says he is concerned if he doesn't live somewhere nice the boys won't want to stay with him, and so he needs the money."

"Great, that makes two of us. How am I supposed to find a place to live in the area if he takes money from the sale? We've done the math. By the time we pay the bank for the current mortgage, the remainder has to go to the next purchase. He's trying to rob me!"

I continued, "This is all because Lillian's client doesn't want to take any money out of his business."

"Well, that is it," Anne agreed. "He told Lillian he doesn't have any visibility on closing dates for current deals, and so he needs a piece from the sale of the flat now."

I shook my head. At least at this point, I could believe it. It is always all about him and his business. "He can't have it both ways. I have to take care of the boys and me. How am I supposed to do that when he is off traveling the world, providing vague dates for any money that might surface?" Suddenly, I realized I was venting. "Right... that's why I am getting a divorce."

Anne said, "Grace, I know it's difficult. I said all this to Lillian, and she suggested perhaps you could get a small mortgage."

"Another mortgage? Fuck him. He wants to provide nothing definite—and then he tells me to take a loan! He wants me to borrow again?"

I could see from their faces that I had crossed the line into crass American. I don't want to alienate my lawyers, and I'd let my language slip. One does not curse in highly respected English solicitor's offices. *This is England, Grace, be civilized!*

For heaven's sake, even when the Queen had two family divorces, the release of a book her daughter-in-law conspired with Andrew Morton to write (*Diana: Her True Story*), and Windsor Castle caught on fire, she referred to it as her "*annus horribilis.*" She did not walk around saying, "This year really sucked." That's something an American would say.

Hmmm, perhaps I need to learn how to say "I married an asshole" in Latin?

I decided I needed to get my language back on track after my lapse from civilized English manners. "Frankly, Anne, even if I wanted to get a mortgage, I don't see how I would qualify for one on my teaching income. Maybe he forgot I didn't work while in chemotherapy. Perhaps you should check to see if Lillian has read a newspaper or watched any TV this year. Maybe she hasn't heard, but banks aren't exactly giving away money these days. Of course, I could explain to the bank that I had cancer and that is why my income was limited—they'll love that. I am sure they will understand. Banks are very understanding places."

Sarcasm had become my substitute for cursing.

Anne responded, "No, Grace, I realize this, and that message has been conveyed."

"The reality is also I am carrying the cost of this litigation, and the more time I spend negotiating with him the less of the insurance money I'll have left," I said.

"Correct, and he has agreed to let you keep the remainder," Anne said.

I refrained from commenting that he should be grateful for the money because it paid for this divorce. As a last-minute peace offering, I tried thinking about the boys we both love so much for a moment.

"Anne, will you tell him I promise to leave all the assets—meaning, my next home—to the boys. Everything I take from this marriage will go to them. I'll put it in my new will. We both have to draw up new wills once we are divorced, and I will make sure everything goes to them. If he wants to see the new will, that is fine with me."

"Okay." Anne cracked open the conference room door. She'd heard all she needed to hear from her annoyed client. She was going back for another round with Lillian. I felt like a boxer in the ring, wondering how many more rounds to go. The difference is I took my hits and bled before I walked into this arena. I have been so cut up and reconstructed across my chest that these rounds felt easy.

Hell, they serve tea and biscuits here. Why, you even get long breaks between rounds—sure beats an operating room. Of course, the best part of having a lawyer is you have a proxy who softens the blows for you. Anne is a good lawyer, because she pushes me to do the work even when I want to quit. Now, however, I have a second wind. I might as well have just looked at Anne and said, "If you tell me this fight is over now, I'll kill you. Get back in there and throw some more punches."

Still, the money issue remained. It loomed large. I don't have a commercial sponsor, and it ain't cheap to run a fight. Ask any Las Vegas casino; a good fight is expensive. I thought, *My soon-to-be ex-husband can afford to be stubborn—I am paying for most of it.*

We returned to waiting, and returned to reflecting. The pain of this divorce is not getting divorced but how I could have tried so very, very hard to succeed at something and failed. Not only did I fail, I refused to see the failure. I kept trying long after the ship sank. Ending the marriage is the relief and the solution.

In the few days leading up to yesterday, we'd been talking. We engaged in actual dialogues, because it was cheaper than paying our lawyers hundreds of pounds an hour to discuss something. This is another small victory in this divorce—his new perspective on my pleas, what he called "complaining" for years.

Another forty minutes passed before Anne returned to the room. Her face was solemn.

"He has agreed to pay all school fees up through university education. He is not budging, however, on taking money from the sale of the flat."

"Did you tell him how I would structure my will?"

"Yes, of course, and he told Lillian he didn't expect anything less from you."

"Well, I expected him to pay university fees. Guess we're even," I said.

Anne replied, "That may be, Grace, but I still think this is a bit of a windfall, as he is not legally required to pay them. Who knows what those fees could be by the time your boys attend university?"

She continued, "I am, however, concerned about your arrangement with the boys. I don't like that they are always with you during the week and him on the weekends. This means he gets all the fun time, and you have to always do homework and school runs."

Anne was right about both, but with Victor's travel schedule I didn't see much choice. My children's university fees were years away. All I could think about was getting a roof over my head immediately.

"I don't see how, with Victor's travel schedule, we can do the living arrangements differently."

I put my head down on the conference table and sighed. I then looked up, addressing both Anne and Nigel, and asked, "Do you think if I give on the money issue we can call it a day?"

"I think so. Grace, let's look at the math. He wants one hundred forty thousand pounds. Even once you pay off the current mortgage, that still leaves you a few hundred thousand."

"Will I be able to get a two bedroom flat in Kensington & Chelsea with that amount?"

"You will probably be forced to consider moving elsewhere or get a mortgage," she conceded. "Because you will be putting a lot of money down, I think you should be able to get a loan."

"Another issue," I said, "is that Thomas takes a school bus now from Kensington to his school. If we move, how will he get there? There are very few bilingual primary schools in this town. Also, we plan to send Rex to the same school."

Another pause, it was really dark outside now.

"How do I know if I agree to this, he won't then try to wiggle more money out of the sale?" I continued, "I am asking because we have not yet completed the sale. What if it falls apart? We are basing our negotiations on this offer. You know there remains the estate agent's fee, property solicitor's fee, my moving costs—it all chips away at what you eventually take from the sale—not to mention stamp duty if I buy somewhere else. That's the real kick."

This time I heard an answer I liked. "Grace, we can structure the settlement so it reads the exact amount he wants, not a penny more."

"How exactly would it read?"

Nigel answered, "Regarding the sale of the flat, the consent order would read whatever the final agreed amount to be paid to him specifically and nothing else. So, taking one hundred forty thousand pounds as the number, we would file with the court a consent order reading: 'One hundred forty thousand pounds to respondent, balance to the petitioner.'"

I paused to digest the information. "Balance to the phoenix, that's what it should say! But that makes sure I receive all that remains outstanding."

"Correct," Anne and Nigel said in unison.

I reflected over the entire offer. It sounds promising, but I question if the word "balance" can ever be used accurately in the same sentence as a "working single mother petitioner."

"So it's twenty thousand pounds a year in spousal support and the remainder of the sale of the flat minus his one hundred forty thousand pounds. He keeps his business. That's his offer."

"Yes."

"I can't live off twenty thousand pounds a year plus my current teaching earnings."

"You can get fifteen percent of any income of his after he pays his expenses, the school, and the nanny for a couple more years. Grace, you've always said you plan to increase your income. There are judges who will award you more, but the problem we have, as we discussed, is your limited resources."

"Meaning I am getting low on cash. What would it cost me to litigate?"

"It depends—a lot. We have discussed this. Nigel would put you in touch with his former firm. They are good and less expensive. I do think, however, with what you have here, you need to consider taking it."

What I also know is if I take this offer, I am still going to have some insurance money left over.

I looked up at both Anne and Nigel. "Okay, I'll do it. One hundred and forty thousand pounds to respondent, balance to the petitioner."

Anne stood up again. "Okay, let me tell Lillian."

After she shut the door, I turned to Nigel, "What time is it?"

"About eight," he answered.

"Thanks. My phone's off, and I didn't want to be staring at a watch today."

"More tea?" he offered, and I accepted. I noticed for the first time all day I was actually a bit hungry.

This time less than fifteen minutes passed before Anne returned. After she shut the door behind her, she said, "Okay, well he has agreed. Lillian and I will have to put it all in writing. Grace, from past experience, there will most likely be something that needs to be clarified, but I do believe we have worked out the makings of a final agreement."

A small pause and I sighed, "Well, I hope so. I really hope it's over."

Nigel then said, "I will work with Lillian to follow up where Anne has left off."

"Okay. How long do you think that will take?" I asked.

"If all goes well, I'll send your draft agreement over in the next couple of weeks," Nigel replied.

They then confirmed I was staying at Phoebe's tonight, as Victor was in the flat. I'd willingly made other arrangements for the evening so he could stay at home the night of this negotiation.

"Yes, I am staying at my friend's place. I am too tired to take the tube. I'm going to call a car service."

"Are you working tomorrow?" Anne asked.

"Yes—not till lunchtime."

"Good," she replied.

A few minutes later, I was alone in the elevator heading to the ground floor. The elevator doors opened. I walked past the law firm's empty reception desk, noticing how much quieter the office had become since I'd arrived this afternoon. All I could hear were the echo-like sounds of my footsteps as I walked across the lobby of this large building with its cavernous lobby. I handed my visitor's pass to the lone night guard at the desk and signed out of the building.

"Evening," was all I said as I left the pass on the round desk and scrawled my name.

A black Volkswagen Sharan waited outside the building for me. Way too big a vehicle for one person, but I decided to value the extra space as I collapsed into the back seat. I needed the space—space alone that I was not negotiating for. I turned on my mobile phone for the first time in eight hours, out of sheer curiosity. I had instructed the babysitter we got to ring the boys' father if necessary today, simply saying I would be unavailable. Today's meeting would not warrant his phone being off for eight hours.

I thought of calling a friend, but I decided I wanted my own company and silence. I looked at the passing streetscape of London and realized that the only thing I know for sure after today is I have made a commitment to this city to be my home. Victor and I both agreed to remain here for the boys.

As the car motored along, I felt enormous relief. Tall orders still await me: supporting myself, taking care of the boys during the week, and watching my health. I know how hard it is to be a single parent; Victor seems to have made me one years ago. I have tried to do it all, and yet this has led to my suffering. Still, I have lived to tell how hard it is. At least I am now leaving a situation that harmed me. I want to stay healthy. I will worry about the rest later.

It also hit me that, with our final agreement, we will have to explain to the boys we are getting divorced—something Victor and I have avoided until now.

1 May 2009 London, Our New Flat

> You all know that security is mortals' chiefest enemy.
> —William Shakespeare, *Macbeth*

A fortnight passed with their father in his new flat and with me packing up ours, and we still had not said anything to the boys. We claimed we were going to have a discussion with them, but, in fact, we both chickened out. I can't speak for their father, but I suspect his reasons are similar to mine—it's too painful. I, for one, have had enough pain and turmoil. I find myself unable to volunteer for more.

Two more weeks pass, and the boys and I moved into the temporary rented flat, just down the road from our old one, that I'd mentioned to the boys over pizza. One unforeseen upside to the banking crisis is that landlords will negotiate. I made offers on three flats, all at one-third less than the landlord's asking price. I made certain to let the estate agents know I had just sold my flat so I am sitting on some cash. All the agents told me their clients would accept the offers.

Our new flat is spacious; the boys like it, and so do I. Again, no questions are asked. I was starting to think we would get away with this.

Then, just yesterday, Thomas told me he couldn't find something. He thinks it may be at his father's place.

"Hey, whose idea was it to get two flats?" he asked.

"Oh, honey, Papa is so tired when he gets off the plane on Thursdays. This way he can get a good night's sleep, so he is all rested on the weekends when he is with you guys."

Thomas looked at me quizzically. I held my breath and hoped this was the end of the conversation. Suddenly, Rex called Thomas from the other room, and he dashed off. Mission accomplished—at least for now.

Madeleine
by Alec Bell

Summer is children,
the world is enticing.
There's life to explore.

The mother who watches
knew summers before.
Gray hair is an ogre
called Anxiety.

Summer is over.
Shadows grow longer
under the trees.

Winter is coming,
now button your coat.
Jack Frost is an ogre
called Maturity.

Madeleine, Madeleine,
bearer of children,
your history binds you
to one single role.
Will you never be whole?

Youth's dance was joyous,
losing stiff selfhood
in blind ecstasy.

Our dancing grew heavy
and swollen with life;

the wet loam of April.
All Fertility.

Under the midnight stars,
he danced with me.
Our seed, deeply planted,
grew vigorously.
My lifeblood fed it,
my Vitality.

Madeleine, Madeleine,
bearer of children,
your history binds you
to one single role.
Will you never be whole?

Frosts of December
grasp the land firmly
in their rigid hold.
Winter's thin fingers
remind you you're old.

You'll soon meet
that ogre, Mortality.

Epilogue 2014

In the years that followed, the boys spent weekdays with me and weekends with their father. My solicitor was right; that proved a difficult way to live. Over a year ago the boys began spending more time with their father, when it became apparent I could no longer continue living that way. Being the homework/school run master took a brutal toll. The boys nicknamed me "Rushy Mama." Their father got all the fun time, and I was left alone on the weekends when most people were spending family time. The writing of this story began as a result of that lifestyle and my weekend solitude.

The boys and I have moved twice since the rental flat. After a year in the rental property, I did buy again and have remained on the property ladder, despite many challenges. It has not been easy. Victor continues to live in South Kensington as always.

The moves proved time-consuming and did not leave me enough time to focus on my teaching career and getting away from the low paying, exploitative adjunct work. At one point I was managing four part-time teaching jobs and was often exhausted. Still, I remain forever grateful I took out those insurance policies and fought a hard-earned battle that led me to be a London homeowner.

I have, however, paid a very high price. My health remains something I need to monitor carefully. I continue to struggle with issues of support. I salute every single mother on the planet who continues to put her individual children's needs as a top priority. (I know many do not.) So many people will never understand the struggle you face. This book is dedicated to you. I only wish we could get more help. I wish it wasn't so hard.

To quote the late American lawyer, writer, and mother Elizabeth Edwards, "*To you I simply say: you know.*"

Acknowledgments

My profound gratitude and thanks to the poet Mr. Alec Bell for all the alchemy he created that transformed a messy manuscript into a coherent memoir. Alec, your editing of my writing is now forever with me. I am fortunate to have found you as a teacher. One of my favorite lessons I love to share with others was your comment, "As Miles Davis said to John Coltrane, you don't have to play every note!"

Further thanks go to Dr. Dennis L. Chapman for introducing me to Alec Bell and whose mastery of the digital universe has helped me get some of my messages out. Your support of my writing and belief I could actually get this polished and published has meant the world to me.

To fellow author Roger Jefferies, even before my brief career as a leg model for *Ursula's Secrets,* you kindly edited chapters. How fortunate both Grace and I were to find in you not only an author but also a fellow lawyer whose professional knowledge helped me better communicate the technical worlds of law and insurance. I now know from my years working on the manuscript alone, no book gets published without the help of creative collaborators, such as you and Alec.

To Dr. Heidi Greiling, for being a friend whose doorstep I can crawl to on the days my usual brisk pace is not an option. Not only do you open that door and your home, but you provide a cup of tea, let me collapse on a sofa, and light a fire in the room I lie in. Our friendship has helped me better understand Jane Austen when she wrote, "Friendship is certainly the finest balm for the pangs of disappointed love."

To my teacher Yogi Ashokanda for helping me attempt mastery of my monkey mind and discovering P.G. McGrath. Thanks to Francesca Quaradeghini for introducing me to yoga. Had I not met you, I would never have found my way to all the incredible places yoga has shown me internally and around the world—from Colleen Saidman Yee's studio in Long Island, New York, to the beaches of the Algarve. More work remains, but thank you for showing me there is another way.

To my other teachers who supported my fabulous formal education, from Dr. Brett Williams at American University to Ellisa Cameron as well as Fordham University's School of Law, you have all contributed to the learning that made me eventually discover the writer within. Also, thanks to my late grandmother, Marion E. McGrath, for her support of my doctorate in jurisprudence.

There are a select group of friends who have supported me in different ways and degrees through the years, no matter what my state, and I thank you in no particular order: Edward J. Dreger, M. Victoria Bayoneto, Crispin Lace, Kristina Kristen, Betsey Campbell Driscoll and Dr. Lauren E. Sheehy.

To all the beautiful students from around the world I have had the joy to teach over the years, while I have changed all your names, some of you may recall discussion points we shared in some of the lecture hall scenes. Please know I think of you all often. While we may no longer have a classroom together, our class remains with me always. You have all taught me so much; thank you.

I extend my thanks to the members of the Richmond Writer's Circle and its chair, Susan Wallbank. You have all been so supportive and provided such great critiques of Grace's journey. I hope you all find some satisfaction in seeing your edits come to life.

Thanks to Jan Cisek and your great design advice.

To the children in my life, starting with my two sons, for reminding me no matter how much I may try as a mother to protect you or filter events, children will draw their own conclusions about what unfolds before them. You are the loves of my life. Also, thanks to Eleanor Ilyas, for teaching me emotional intelligence has nothing to do with age.

With gratitude and love,
P. G. McGrath
London, May 2014

Lightning Source UK Ltd.
Milton Keynes UK
UKOW02f0411200814

237221UK00002B/79/P